WISDOM FROM A WATCHMAN

BY JACK FERGUSON

Published by:

HAYES PRESS

The Barn, Flaxlands

Royal Wootton Bassett

Swindon, SN4 8DY

United Kingdom

WWW.HAYESPRESS.ORG

First Edition June 2016

10 9 8 7 6 5 4 3 2 1

CHAPTER ONE: LET NO MAN TAKE THY CROWN

———

T here were times when kings went out to battle. It was "at the return of the year" and many a time David went out with the host and ably fought the battles of the Lord. In those contests he earned for himself an imperishable name in the age-long records of the people of God.

The Lord's enemies were David's enemies and he gave them no quarter. He knew where to draw the line between friend and foe and with that line he measured all who opposed his God. Moab knew something of that line in 2 Samuel 8. David had a "no compromise" battle cry.

Nor should we forget that David's battles had spiritual issues, for the spoil of war became the dedicated things of the house of the LORD. The whole bent of David's mind and the entire direction of his immense energies were towards the building and beautifying of a house worthy of a God so majestic as Jehovah of Hosts.

But lightning often strikes the tallest buildings first, and the higher the building the greater the fall. So one fateful day David tarried at home when he should have been vigorously setting off in pursuit of the purposes of God. Instead he let others go, and Joab in particular. And one brief consequent indulging of the flesh brought a sword into his family for ever.

Christian, these are days for hot pursuit of the enemy and for the advancement of the kingdom of God. No-compromising days of private witness, soul seeking and soul winning; praying others into the kingdom. Days for collective effort by the Lord's people, working amongst young folk, in open-air testimony, in tract distribution and many other lines of attack. Shun, above all else that you shun, the weakening inroads of self-indulgence. Ask the Lord to make you a healthy-minded, vigorous conqueror, who can do all things through Him who strengthens you. The devil will leave unclean things lying around beside you where you work. Ask God on the spot for strength not to weaken to take them up. Other temptations will be presented to you, but each victory will help you some other to win. Again the poet wrote:

"From silken self, O Captain, free

Thy soldier, who would follow Thee.

From subtle love of softening things

From easy choices, weakenings,

Not thus are spirits fortified,

Not this way went the Crucified,

From all that dims Thy Calvary,

O Lamb of God, deliver me."

So David tarried and Joab was sent forth. The battle was at the gate of Rabbah, capital of the king of the Ammonites. The battle plan was set for the taking of the royal city. It was well within Joab's striking distance. But whatever else Joab may have been he was, for the most part, a man of unswerving loyalty to David. And, nobly, he sent word to his royal leader that day to come and personally to take the city, not to be deprived of the honour of taking the king's crown which weighed a talent of gold and was set with precious stones. So David came, and of that same crown it is written, "And it was set on David's head." Yes, it was, thanks to the mercy of God, through the loyalty of Joab, whose message to David had virtually been "Let no man take thy crown."

Crowns at stake today - what a thought! Some failing of the saints' reward! Others passing in with an abundant entrance! This morning, after the Breaking of the Bread, a brother was ministering regarding some of the earlier apostles who laid down their lives in the savage martyrdom of pitiless, relentless Rome. Yet to these same apostles the word of the Lord had come, "and when the Son of Man shall sit on the throne of His glory, ye also shall sit upon twelve thrones, judging the twelve tribes of Israel." Yes, it was their firm conviction that better to lose their head, than to lose their crown.

Christian, do not let self-indulgence weaken you in the race so that you lose your crown in that day of reward, nor let any other pursuit in life deflect you from the path of surrender to your Lord's will, nor yet let any kind of self-effacement hinder you from taking your due part in the Lord's work. "In honour preferring one another" hasn't the meaning which some shelter behind. It means rather, in honourable things leading one another on - on towards the crown.

And should you see another brother (or sister) in danger of losing the crown, remember Joab and the crown of the royal city, and prayerfully put your arm through theirs and seek to draw them again closer to the heavenly Captain and to the battle at the gate.

CHAPTER TWO: A QUESTION OF DUTY

———

It all arose out of the Lord's word regarding forgiveness in Luke 17. It seemed to the apostles to place altogether excessive demands upon them. It was not the first time He had spoken on the subject. Very early in His ministry He had taught the disciples that there was no point in asking their heavenly Father for forgiveness if they themselves were not prepared to forgive others. On another occasion He had told them that so vast was the debt their Father had forgiven them, that any forgiveness shown by them to others was small by contrast. But now the word was even more explicit and expansive.

"Take heed to yourselves: if thy brother sin, rebuke him; and if he repent, forgive him. And if he sin against thee seven times in the day, and seven times turn again to thee, saying, I repent; thou shalt forgive him". It is the only time that the apostles are recorded as replying in unison to the Lord. They said, "Increase our faith". But the Lord pointed out that this was not a question of faith, it was one of duty. First rebuke the brother who has wronged you. But then, if he expresses his regret, forgive him. Thereafter there is to be no limit to recurrence of the procedure.

It brought from the Lord a very interesting parable on the subject of the sense of duty which prompted response to His commandments. He referred to the farmer who engages a servant to plough and to keep the sheep. At the close of the day it was not a question of the farmer calling the servant in from the field to the evening meal and attending first to his needs. Indeed it was just the reverse. "Even so ye also, when ye shall have done all the things that are commanded you, say, 'We are unprofitable servants; we have done that which it was our duty to do.'"

Ploughing and keeping sheep - there is something very akin to this in our own commandments from the Lord. We have an outgoing commission to take the message of life and the word of truth to others. This "ploughing" is very, very often hard and seeming unrewarding work. Talks with neighbours, friends and colleagues; Bible messages from door to door; teaming up with brothers and sisters for outreach work. The servants of the Lord still plough in the steadfast hope of reaping someone, some day: still sow in tears in the dauntless faith that sheaves will yet be gathered in.

We have also the continual demands of assembly life. Sometimes it is hard going, this matter of "keeping sheep". Caring for one another; avoiding offence; visiting the afflicted; constant in attendance while others seem to sit on the perimeter; some brothers in perpetual exercise; others with their talent hidden away; well instructed sisters maintaining their subjection, though irksome many a time. But our Master says that this is the path of duty. Sometimes we chafe our spirits, questioning our motives in all this. Are we doing it "for love's sake"? Well indeed when it is so. But the plain fact remains, that we have received certain specific commands from our absent Lord and in our loyalty to Him it is our unremitting duty to respond.

Then one day, at even-time, we shall all go in together from ploughing and keeping sheep. And on our way to whatever place of service may be assigned to us in infinite grace in the eternal Kingdom, we shall stay a little while at His Judgement-seat. Please God, we shall come there, in spite of all our failures, in that sense of accomplishment envisaged in verse 10 of our chapter, "Even so ye also, when ye shall have done all the things that are commanded you". And already, as it were, the Master has taught us what to be ready to say at the conclusion of our giving of account: 'We are unprofitable servants; we have done that which it was our duty to do.'

Amy Carmichael, you may remember, wrote very beautifully about India and duty:

When each duty crowds the other

Through the sultry days,

Plant the little flower of patience

By our ways.

When the slothful flesh would murmur,

Ease would cast her spell,

Set our face as flint till twilight's

Vesper bell.

On Thy brow we see a thorn-crown,

Blood-drops in Thy track,

O forbid that we should ever

Turn us back.

CHAPTER THREE: RENT HEARTS

———

Rent hearts mean rent heavens. Israel cried, through Isaiah, "Oh that Thou wouldest rend the heavens, that Thou wouldest come down." The LORD spoke through Joel, "Rend your heart and not your garments, and turn unto the LORD your God." There was only one pathway to blessing, then and now. It was by the rent heart.

It was an old custom in Israel, and indeed among the nations, to rend the garments in a time of sorrow. But very largely it came to be a token of sorrow only, an outward expression of no real inward grief! Hence when Jehoram, king of Israel, passed by upon the wall and heard from the frenzied woman the outcome of sin in the nation he rent his clothes "and the people looked, and behold, he had sackcloth within upon his flesh." But he had no sackcloth on his heart, for "he cleaved unto the sins of Jeroboam ... he departed not therefrom." It would have been much more profitable for himself and the nation if he had rent his heart and not his garments.

God abhors external expressions where there is no corresponding inward grace. Christian, we must avoid cold, empty formalism. You know the kind of thing - attending the gatherings of the Lord's people, but with no real interest at heart. Meeting with the saints on Lord's day, but silent in testimony and perhaps even of a doubtful testimony through the week. Going to the assembly prayers, but the private prayer life all dried up, or the assembly scripture reading and no meditative reading at home. We all know the symptoms; we have all had them at one time or another. But they displease the Lord and hinder blessing.

"Rend your heart," saith the Lord, "and not your garments." Are we not longing among the assemblies of God today for reviving and a definite outpouring of divine blessing? How seldom it is said abroad today that "God hath visited His people." Surely the Lord's hand is not shortened that it cannot save! Surely the risen Conqueror of Calvary has not foregone the victory and the honour and the glory which are His! No, the trouble lies in our own un-rent hearts.

Apathy among Christians is the present day master-stroke of the devil. What greater tragedy can you imagine than a brand, plucked from the burning, completely indifferent to the needs of other brands, who are thoughtlessly preparing themselves for the eternal burnings? Or saints who have seen the light and the way to the City, caring nothing for the multitudes of believers who have missed that same way to the house of God, and who are contenting themselves in evangelical outlets for their zeal? Once the adversary sees a people right for God positionally, he will use every endeavour to make them wrong for God conditionally. He will readily achieve that through apathy and spiritual indifference.

Brothers and sisters, let us return to the Lord with rent hearts and confess that we have been unprofitable servants and that much divine grace has been received by us in vain. "Search me,

O God, and know my heart; try me, and know my thoughts; and see if there be any way of wickedness in me, and lead me in the way everlasting." And following these individual words of David, Jeremiah wrote nationally, "Let us search and try our ways, and turn again to the LORD."

Rent hearts bring whole tithes. Whole tithes involve yielded lives. These may claim the promise of the opened windows of heaven pouring down the blessing. Can you think of a place or a people more appropriate to the fulness of divine blessing than the people of God in churches of God? Even as it is written "and I will make them and the places round about My hill a blessing"; saith the LORD. Beyond question the Lord is blessing, in His sovereignty, beyond the borders of His gathered-out people to-day. It may be that others are rending their hearts while we are simply still rending our garments. It may be others are bringing the whole tithe while some of us are keeping back part of the price. Well then did the old paraphrase say, "Come let us to the Lord our God, with contrite hearts return."

Fellow-Christian, shall we pray about this?

CHAPTER FOUR: YIELDED!

———

S ay, fellow-Christian, "Know ye not, that to whom ye present yourselves as servants unto obedience, his servants ye are whom ye obey; whether of sin unto death, or of obedience unto righteousness?" Well does the Holy Spirit say, "Yield yourselves unto God" (Romans 6.13 KJV).

The yielded life! It sounds passive. Actually it is gloriously active over sin. Somebody has to reign within us and enjoy priority in our ways. It will either be God in righteousness or the Devil in sin. To whom then are we yielding ourselves? It must be the One or the other.

Daniel's three companions are deathless examples of the yielded life. Nebuchadnezzar demanded that he reign within and that the young men should manifest this in the worship of his image. To refuse meant roasting to death in a sevenfold-heated furnace of flame. But these three young noblemen of faith trusted in God, changed the king's word, and yielded their bodies that they might serve no god other than their own God. Young men like these turn worlds upside down.

"Ye cannot serve God and mammon." To one or other we must yield ourselves. Which is it going to be? Mammon and the pleasures of sin? Surely not! You know, Christian, that the Devil has a well-ordered world around us, cunningly calculated to blind men to eternal things. It fascinates the unsaved. It holds the way of sport for the gratification of playing the game or

watching it, or getting on it. It is all self, all mammon. It ap-
plauds the way of culture, the improvement of the human mind
through the arts and the sciences. It is all transient and passing,
nothing eternal or abiding; all mammon. It blazes the door-
ways to entertainment and the pleasures of sin, highbrow or
lowdown. It is all mammon again, nothing for God or the Man
of Calvary. These are the things of which we became ashamed
in the day we trusted Him. Surely then the Lord is not going to
have to say of us as He said of Israel, "He feedeth on ashes: a deceived heart hath turned him aside." A deceived heart! Again
the Scriptures echo, "The Devil that deceived them."

No! Rather would there come to us that ancient and clarion
call that has rung in the souls of Christians down twenty centuries of twisted time, setting them on fire for the Lord and
burning up the chaff of indolent ways: "Neither present (that
is, keep on presenting) your members unto sin as instruments
of unrighteousness; but present yourselves unto God, as alive
from the dead." Yes, once and for all, present yourselves - yielded to God. "And so I charge you by the thorny crown, and by
the cross on which the Saviour bled, and by your own soul's
hope of fair renown ..." yield yourselves.

"Dead unto sin" is glorious truth, but negative in effect. "Alive
unto God" is both positive and effectual. What a joy to the
Lord to see Christians with the forward look and the Calvary
love! Not hankering after the old life, but pressing on, thrilled
with the new, abundantly satisfied with the river of God's pleasures and the fatness of His house. Presenting their "bodies a
living sacrifice," or a sacrifice of life. Yes, surrendering their lives
to Him with all their vigour and zest; keeping back no part of

the price, but bringing it all forward - time, talents and all. Miss Havergal enumerates "life, moments, days, hands, feet, voice, lips, silver, gold, intellect, power, will, heart, love" - and finally – "Take myself, and I will be ever, only, all for Thee."

Some are holding back today, some are looking back, some are shrinking back, some are going back. In ways like these the Lord can have no pleasure. It is only a little time till "He that cometh shall come, and shall not tarry." Only a little longer to walk by faith; only a little longer to read and study His Word, to commune by faith in prayer, to give out our silent messengers, to speak a word for Him, to bear patiently for His Name's sake and not grow weary, to walk the way of good men and of good works. Yes, "one little hour; and then the glorious crowning, the golden harp-strings and the victor's palm; one little hour; and then the 'Hallelujah,' Eternity's long, deep thanksgiving psalm." The church -presented to Him for ever!

Fellow-Christian, be entreated for His Name's sake, and yield yourself to-day, surrendered to Him.

CHAPTER FIVE: THE FEAR OF THE LORD

———

O ne address which remains with me from early youth was that of the Lord's day afternoon following the sudden homegoing of a man in the assembly. It was from Psalm 12. "Help, LORD, for the godly man ceaseth." Godly men seemed to be ceasing then. They had been ceasing in the Psalmist's day also. They are ceasing still. They constantly cease, but have hitherto been continually replaced. If the adversary can destroy this process of replenishing the ranks of the godly he will be well satisfied. The battle then is on and raging furiously.

The fear of the LORD is still the beginning of wisdom. We have learned that truth from Solomon. His father David taught it to him and it runs like a golden thread through the book of Proverbs. Nor was it only his son to whom David taught this truth. He taught it also to the loyal band which separated themselves to him to the cave of Adullam. Many a time you may have wondered what they talked about in the long evenings in the cave. Psalm 34 helps us. David wrote that Psalm after he had fled from Abimelech, and 1 Samuel 22 tells us that it was then that he retreated to the cave. So he gathered his helpers in war around him. He would have to train them. Those of most use to him would learn to sling with both hands, "at an hairbreadth and not miss." But a still more vital matter must have precedence in the school of the cave. "Come, ye children hearken unto me," said David, "I will teach you the fear of the LORD." That then was the conversation of the cave, later also it was the conversation of the Palace and many humbler homes in Israel besides.

This matter of the fear of the LORD had always been held by some and then passed on in Israel from one generation to another. It was part of the rich heritage; a sort of barometer also of home and national life. For example, Abraham confessed mistakenly one day that the fear of God was not in the place to which his erring feet had taken him. So he turned back penitent. He must learn, perhaps the hard way, to be a companion of all them that fear God, otherwise only sorrow would ensue. You will read of this in Genesis 20.

Abraham's son Isaac must in turn have drunk deeply of his father's wholesome godly fear, for the impression of God which rooted itself early in the mind of his son Jacob was that He was "the Fear of his father Isaac." Isaac had lived the home life of a god-fearing man.

And Jacob taught his boy Joseph, in his first tender seventeen years, so thoroughly to fear God that when the Devil pressed hard upon him one day, through the immoral suggestions of a wicked woman, he fled from the temptress, crying, "How then can I do this great wickedness and sin against God?" He had learned to fear God and that fear made him hate sin. You will find Genesis 39. profitable reading, in company with 1 Timothy 6.11-12.

They taught each other in those days the fear of the LORD. To them it was the very beginning of wisdom and we pass it on

today. Schooling days, apprenticeship days, evening class studies - these may all be pressing at the moment, for there is still
no royal road to learning. But above all that you learn, learn to
fear God. In the measure in which you fear Him you will hate
sin. "The fear of the LORD is clean," said David, "enduring for
ever." And as you learn it you will say with Joseph, when the
tempter from beneath spreads his wares, "How then can I do
this great wickedness and sin against God?"

A devout man once said, "If Satan comes up to my door, I cannot help it; if he lifts the latch and walks in, I cannot help it.
But if I offer him a chair and begin with him a parley, I put myself altogether in the wrong." Sin still couches at the door of
those who neglect to fear God; couches with a fearful power to
master the unwary.

Holland's first defence against the century-old tidal menace is
the sand dunes. They have little defensive value in their natur-
al state, but a special kind of grass is sown in them, the roots
of which form an entangled network acting as binder. Where
there are no dunes the Dutch have built three main series of
dykes. The first of these is called the Watchman, the second the
Sleeper, the third the Dreamer. The tides of sin roll relentless-
ly too, longing to break through and ravage. Our first dyke, the
Watchman, is the fear of the Lord. Hewn on a stone on the
Zuiderzee Dyke, twenty miles long, are the words "A nation
that lives builds for its future." Keep that first dyke high in your
life, Christian. Your whole future usefulness for the beloved
Master depends upon it. "Fear God."

The fear of the LORD makes for communion. Sin only breaks communion. And as for conscious sin, well did a last-century preacher thunder out that it is "a clenched fist, an outstretched arm, a blow aimed at the face of Almighty God." Wholesome then is the counsel of Solomon in Proverbs 20.17: "Let not thine heart envy sinners; but be thou in the fear of the LORD all the day long." This is the sort of spiritual atmosphere in which Christians will prosper. For that reason we should shun places and company where His Name is not feared. Malachi 3.16 shows us that the God-fearing seek each other out and talk together, and those conversations high Heaven hears. Truly, mutual God-fearingness is a perfect basis for companionship, as the Psalmist expressed in Psalm 119.16: "I am a companion of all them that fear Thee."

The fear of the LORD will produce within us also that "reverence and awe" with which we must learn to serve God in His House. Should we not live every day in the light of the drawing near on Lord's day morning? Should we not keep ourselves from sin, by the Lord's help, having in mind the entry into the Holy Place with the holy priesthood at the breaking of the bread? And at the gatherings of God's people when you have taken your seat, reverently bow your head and concentrate on the purpose of the gathering. Do not look around you during the service. Remember that in spirit you have drawn near. You are in the Presence. "Be thou in the fear of the LORD."

In His stoop to manhood, the Lord Jesus in His youth feared God in a way we shall never appreciate. And in all the fervency of His prayer-life His godly fear was a nightly experience with God. You will recollect what Hebrews 5.7 says on the point.

Fellow-disciple, model your life, God helping you, on the life of the Lord Jesus. Shun, as He did, pride, self-assertion, temper and the self-centred life. Hate sin in your inward parts. Fear God in your heart and the issues of your life will be clean, delightful to your fellows and well-pleasing to the Lord.

"Fear God" said the Holy Spirit in 1 Peter 2.17.

"Yea, I say unto you," said the Lord Jesus in Luke 12.5, "FEAR HIM."

Shall we echo the song of the singers by the glassy sea, coming victorious from the beast and from his image, and from the number of his name? "Who shall not fear Thee, O Lord for Thou only art holy?" For His Name's sake.

CHAPTER SIX: REST AND REMEMBER

This was the purpose of the Sabbath in Israel. Every seventh day the Israelite did no work, nor any of his servants or his animals, "that thy manservant and thy maidservant may rest as well as thou. And thou shalt remember that thou wast a servant in the land of Egypt (Deut. 5.14,15). They were to rest and remember.

God has blessed that day and hallowed it, for in six days He Himself had made heaven and earth, the sea and everything in them; then He rested on the seventh day. Not that He required rest, who "fainteth not neither is weary". It was more probably the rest of satisfaction in a perfectly completed work. And not only did He rest, but He was "refreshed" (Ex. 31.17). So in relation to that rest He established also a principle, which all people everywhere, and in every generation would do well to follow. The One who formed the human frame knew the renewing, the refreshing that would come from a weekly physical rest and spiritual reflection. And today, some 3,500 years later, the people of God still need a day in which to rest, to remember and to be refreshed.

Justin is thought to be one of the earliest, authentic writers in the years which immediately followed the period of the New Testament apostles and prophets. He gives with considerable minuteness an account of the services held by the early Christians on the first day of the week, the Lord's day. So although the original nucleus of the New Testament churches was a Jewish remnant according to the election of grace, embracing of course an ever-increasing number of Gentiles as the work expanded, the early Christians attached so unique a significance to the first day of the week that it replaced the Sabbath as the day of their special spiritual exercises. It was the resurrection day, the day of the new order, the Lord's unique day.

It all began on that memorable "When therefore it was evening, on that day, the first day of the week ..." (John 20.19). Again, seven weeks later, on the first day of the week, "When the day of Pentecost was now come, they were all together in one place" (Acts 2.1). Later, "Upon the first day of the week let each one of you lay by him in store" (1 Cor. 16.2). And subsequently, "And upon the first day of the week, when we were gathered together to break bread ..." (Acts 20.7).

The transition from the observance by the Jews of the Sabbath to the recognition by the early Christians of the first day of the week could not have been easy. The Sabbath had been "made for man" (Mark 2.27) but it was also "unto the LORD" (Deut. 5.14). To the Jew the Sabbath was the normal day of rest. To the Jewish Christian the first day of the week was for the service of the Lord. This may well have meant that for a considerable time many of the disciples would not be free till the evening of the Lord's day. Indeed the reference to the Lord's supper in 1 Corinthians 11.20 and the prolonged discourse of Paul till midnight (Acts 20.7) may have a bearing on this. But in any event, they held fast to the new arrangement and in due course the first day of the week became the Christian's day for rest to them and service to God.

What a lovely arrangement, approved by the Lord for this period of grace, to have one day in the week set apart by the "Israel of God" for the refreshment which comes from rest and remembrance! A day disturbed only by the minimum of normal everyday engagements, when we can experience in a special way the joyful Christian paradox of which the Lord Jesus spoke, "Take My yoke upon you ... and ye shall find rest unto your souls" (Matt. 11.29). Rest, in the activity of the service of God.

And not only rest, but remembrance. It was a marvellous forethought on God's part to call us to the breaking of the bread on the first day of the week. And if "On that day did David make it the chief work to give thanks unto the LORD" (1 Chron. 16.7 RV margin), is it any wonder that the Spirit has guided us to keep the Remembrance first thing on the Lord's day?

This is the service of perennial freshness. Week by week the Spirit stirs our memories with new appreciations of the Lord Jesus, drawn from the shadows of the Old Testament, from the unfoldings of the New. We meditate on Galilee, Gethsemane, Golgotha - we remember Him, who brought us from the bondage of sin into the glory of the freedom of the service of God. Thoughts form in inward worship, in outward praise. And from the Remembrance we turn again homeward, refreshed for rest in further service. Further service, that is, to others. In infinite grace we have been shown the excellencies of Him who called us out of darkness into His marvellous light. Ora Rowan in "Idols" caught the thought:

Hast thou heard Him, seen Him, known Him?

Is not thine a captured heart?

Chief among the thousands own Him,

Gladly choose the better part.

Others are still in darkness, blinded. To these we must go, to the young, to the mature. And there are lonely friends to call on or invite along to tea. There are sick ones to be visited, wayward feet to be tended.

Yes, there must always be something unique about the Lord's day to the Lord's people. It carries a sanctification to the things of the Spirit which reaches its ultimate in being "in the Spirit on the Lord's day" (Rev. 1.10). The impact of the spirit of the age is adverse and unrelenting. It brings in all its subtlety a strong temptation to many to take on unnecessary Sunday work, to catch up on a host of domestic chores, to concentrate on college studies, to the detriment of the King's business. We will be a stronger people for God if we make it our custom to go in for the refreshment which comes from His service on the first day of the week, and on that day also to rest and remember.

Maybe some brother or sister reading these lines is too old or too sick or for some other valid reason too tied to be able to gather with the Lord's people as once you used to and now would long to. It is Lord's day morning. How choice if you could think about the disciple whom Jesus loved, now John the aged, banished to Patmos for his Master's sake. And on that memorable Lord's day morning he would look across the Aegean Sea in the direction of the Ephesus he loved. And as he mused on earlier, happy days there among the disciples he would think of them at that moment, gathered together to break bread. He would remember the old hymns, the old faces. And gently and silently he "was in the Spirit on the Lord's day".

CHAPTER SEVEN: MARKED FOREHEADS

———

On Aaron's forehead was a golden plate for all to see, day after day. It was held in place by a lace of blue on the forefront of the mitre, his priestly head-dress. On the golden plate were engraved the awesome words, HOLY TO THE LORD. The message to the nation was that their high priest bore the iniquity of the holy things. Someone was needed to reconcile the iniquity in the offerers with the holiness of their gifts. The deeper truth was that God saw in the priesthood of Aaron shadows of the coming priesthood of His Son and in this way He was able to bear with Israel's failure in the service of His house (Ex. 28.36-38).

We are not pursuing here the typical teaching of the mitre with its golden plate and lace of blue. We are thinking simply of a man walking about every day, in the presence of God, in the company of the people outside, and on his forehead was this testimony to personal consecration - HOLY TO THE LORD.

The forehead stands related to personal characteristics in various ways in Scripture. For example, King Uzziah had a leprous forehead, indicating an inward condition of pride and deliberate trespass against the Lord (2 Chron. 26.19).

Israel in her national depravity was described by God as having "a whore's forehead". She had completely lost her early love for the Lord and gone after the meaningless idols of the nations (Jer. 3.3).

Ezekiel, dedicated to taking the word of the Lord to rebellious Israel, had, metaphorically, his forehead made "as an adamant harder than flint" so that he could stand against a people who were "of an hard forehead and of a stiff heart" (Ezek. 3.7-9).

The Hebrew word translated forehead is rooted in the thought of 'clear' or 'prominent'. Thus from the Old Testament allusions the message comes to us today in all its power. Clearly evident in our lives, prominent for all to see, should be a sense of being "holy to the LORD", avoiding pride and trespass against Him, strong in our desire not to let our hearts wander after tawdry priorities, and determined in our defence of the faith.

In the New Testament there are two extremely unpleasant instances of marked foreheads. In the tribulation period those who, against all divine warning, stand boldly and impudently for the worship of the first beast of Revelation 13, and his image, will doubtless be those who receive his mark on their forehead; others on their hand. This will be their authority from the man of sin for a brief period of trading but at the fearful cost of their eternal doom (Rev. 13.16,17; 14.9-12).

John also saw that on the forehead of the woman sitting on the scarlet-coloured beast was a name written: "Mystery, Babylon the great, the mother of the harlots and of the abominations of the earth". The name is indicative of her character; the woman herself of the vast ecumenical movement, already in evidence today, but to be thrust into violent momentum by the departure of every born again person at the Rapture.

With joyful, contrasting relief we turn to other marked foreheads in the New Testament. Again they are in the Revelation. First the 144,000; the seal on their foreheads indicating that they are the servants of God (Rev. 7.3; 9.4). Then another group of the same number are seen standing with the Lamb on the heavenly Mount Zion. These, in their dedication, follow the Lamb wherever He goes. And His name and that of His Father are written on their foreheads (Rev. 14.1-5).

But what shall we say of Revelation 22:4? There, in the New Jerusalem, "His servants shall do Him service; and they shall see His face; and His name shall be on their foreheads". What an ultimate for the disciple! What a sublime prospect for us all! Assigned to a place in the service of the everlasting kingdom; looking for ever on the King's face: marked as His for the eternal day of God.

Is it not worth-while to be a known disciple today? To be men and women of the marked foreheads.

CHAPTER EIGHT: ON THE HOLY MOUNT

———

There have been many holy scenes on Bible mountains but never one like this. It is recounted in Matthew 17.1-8; Mark 9.2-8 and Luke 9.28-36. The background is deeply significant. It was away in the north at Caesarea Philippi, on the border of Gentile territory. There, apparently for the first time, the Lord Jesus unfolded His plan to build a Church which in later days would be found to embrace both Jews and Gentiles. But the cost would be His own life. So immediately following this He disclosed explicitly to His followers that His earthly journey would culminate in a death of suffering to be followed by His return to glory.

Then he invited individual disciples to follow Him in His path through suffering to glory. He put it to them in that characteristic manner which since then many have learned to love. He said, in effect, "For your sakes I must go that way. Are any of you willing to follow Me?'"

With this he linked the memorable threefold reason why His disciples should follow Him, concluding with the promise that certain of those standing around would "in no wise taste of death, till they see the Son of Man coming in His kingdom" (Matthew), or "till they see the kingdom of God come with power" (Mark). Some understand this as the establishing of the kingdom of God at Pentecost. Others see the fulfilment in the Transfiguration scene which followed six days later.

But however this may be viewed, the background to the Transfiguration is clearly the Lord's explicit announcement of His suffering and death at the hands of the leaders of Israel. All heaven was evidently interested in the subject. It was so at His birth also, when an angel brought the tidings. But it was two men, Moses and Elijah, who were sent down to talk about His death. These men stand related in the ways of God to the original constitution and the ultimate restoration of Israel respectively. They represented the law and the prophets.

It was night on the Holy Mount. The three apostles must have been forever grateful that they did not sleep through all those memorable hours. The Lord had been praying in His usual way, when suddenly He was transfigured before them. His whole appearance was altered to the brightness of the sun in its full strength, and His garments became white as the light. Then in their own relative glory came Moses and Elijah from heaven to commune with Him. No wonder Michael, the archangel, had a dispute with the devil about the body of Moses. No wonder a chariot and horses of fire accompanied Elijah as he went up by a whirlwind into heaven. These men were to come back later in the service of God.

Together, for a little while, they spoke of "His decease which He was about to accomplish at Jerusalem". Had Luke not told us this, the subject of the conversation would doubtless have provided endless, inconclusive discussion among Christians. They talked about His death, His departure to the Father, the exodus He would lead as a kind of firstfruits, which would far exceed what Moses had led from Egypt.

The disciples were not yet ready to receive the implications of His impending death, but all heaven awaited it, for the counsels of eternity required it, and messengers had come from heaven to strengthen Him for it. The law and the prophets had abundantly predicted it and now their representatives attended in person to bow out of the scene and allow the Son of God to fill it with His own glory.

Then the disciples saw the heavenly messengers about to leave. The grandeur of the whole scene had made them afraid. Peter felt something appropriate was called for, so blurted out the suggestion that they should all remain together and they would make three booths for the Lord, for Moses and for Elijah. But while he was still speaking, one of God's great clouds enveloped them (how often the divine presence was associated with clouds!) and the voice from heaven came to them, "This is My beloved Son, My Chosen, in whom I am well pleased; hear ye Him".

Little wonder the disciples fell on their faces, sore afraid. Then they felt a touch, heard the familiar voice say, "Arise, and be not afraid". And there He stood beside them, "Jesus only", the same Jesus they knew and loved so well.

Years later Peter recounted it all in his second letter, see 2 Pet. 1.16-21. If the whole enactment on the holy mount brought strength to his Master for His coming encounter, it clearly brought also to Peter a sense of spiritual stability which was to fortify him for the years of his ministry.

Thereafter no one would ever persuade him that he had mistakenly followed "cunningly devised fables". There on the mount he had actually been an eyewitness of the presence of the Lord Jesus Christ in majesty and power. He had actually heard the voice of God giving honour and glory to the Son of His pleasure. He had actually witnessed the representatives of the law and the prophets speaking with the One whose coming they had long foretold.

So to Peter in that day, and to us in ours, the seal was set to the whole word of Old Testament prophecy. Now it shines in all its brilliance like a lamp in a dark place, and will continue to do so till the Light Himself breaks through the gloom at His coming. Till which day, says Peter, we do well to take heed in our hearts to that same sure Word.

CHAPTER NINE: THE PLEADER

———

The law courts of the nations have heard impassioned appeals by brilliant pleaders. Juries have been swayed. Judges may have been affected. These men had power with the human mind.

In Bible history, too, there have been pleaders. But these men, to use Hosea's expression, "had power with God ... and prevailed". This was pleading at its highest level; profound pleading with God on behalf of Israel (as in the case of Moses, our present study), or, contrariwise, against them (as in the case of Elijah). These were the supplications of righteous men, which, James tells us, availed much in their working. They were the effectual pleadings of fervent prayer.

These men knew their God. Their intercessions were keenly intelligent in their understanding of the divine will, daring in their demand, brilliant in their presentation. Clearly God loved to be appealed to by such men. And women, too. Take for an example of intelligent intercession Hannah's prayer for the needs of God in His holy temple. "O LORD of hosts ... give unto Thine handmaid a man child" (1 Sam. 1.11). "LORD of hosts" - never before in Scripture had this Name reached His ear. It was a woman, reminding Him that He had hosts and she only wanted one. God loved such intelligence in intercession.

Only some three months had passed since Israel was led out in joy from Egypt, and already they were returning in heart to it. They had pledged themselves to the covenant of obedience and for the fifth time Moses climbed Sinai. He went as Israel's mediator, to receive on their behalf the living oracles, the ordinance of angels. Little did he realize the dual form his mediation would take.

But God knew, for "known unto God are all His works from the beginning of the world" (Acts 15.18 KJV). If we could foresee the end of certain courses of action we would never embark on them. We would shrink from failure. But not so the omniscient God. "From the beginning of the world" He has known that enemies will assail His plans and friends will fail in their assignments. Yet nothing deflects Him from His purposes, nor affects His zeal in offering opportunities to men to serve Him. Were it not so He would never initiate any project for the benefit of humankind.

And so it was in the matter of the golden calf. God took Israel at their word in Exodus 24 though He knew they would worship the calf in a matter of days. He gave Moses the pattern of the Tabernacle with the details of the priestly garments and service, knowing that even while He was speaking, Aaron was leading the nation into idolatry. But His prescience of failure was not allowed to affect the sweetness of the forty days' communion with Moses.

The conduct of the nation at the foot of the mountain was incomprehensible. They had seen the signs in Egypt, the miracle of the Red Sea; they had heard the voice of the living God from the fires of Sinai. All we can say is, "let him that thinketh he standeth take heed lest he fall". They insisted on the tangible. From the first day Moses knew them they were a people void of faith. Right at the outset they failed in the test of his absence. Their hearts went back to Egypt and its gods. So Aaron took their gold, made a calf for them to worship, and incongruously linked the service with a feast to the Lord. Round the idol they danced in an orgy of loose permissiveness, to what Dr. Strong describes in his concordance as "the scornful whispering (of hostile spectators)".

When their communion was over, God told Moses to leave His presence, for the people whom he (Moses) had brought from Egypt had turned aside to corrupted ways. God just wished to be alone so that His anger might wax hot. Moses was still unaware of the details of the corruption. All he knew was that the fate of the nation was already in the balance with God. To borrow the famous words of Jonathan Edwards in another context, Israel had fallen "into the hands of an angry God". He wished to destroy them completely and to start afresh with Moses.

Through him He would maintain unbroken the covenant of Abraham of the seed and the land, just as through Noah he had maintained the promise of the woman's Seed. But centuries later they sang in Israel that on that day "Moses His chosen stood before Him in the breach, to turn away His wrath, lest He should destroy them" (Ps. 106.23). Later in Israel's history God said, "And I sought for a man among them, that should make up the fence, and stand in the gap before Me for the land, that I should not destroy it: but I found none" (Ezek. 22.30). But in the day of the golden calf, Moses the pleader was there to stand in the breach.

His intercession was brief, intelligent, demanding. It was the perfect plea which could not go unanswered. It had three points. The first was that Israel was the Lord's own espoused people, redeemed by such great power. The second was how Egypt would mock the glory of God were He to destroy the people He had just delivered. The third was a nostalgic remembrance of covenant promises to the patriarchs. Again there was as it were a hand "lifted up upon the throne of Jah" (Ex. 17.16 Hebrew marg.), and the judgement was stayed.

Then Moses came down and saw for himself the reason for the divine wrath and his own anger waxed hot in turn. He burned the golden calf in the fire (the secret of which remarkable process he may have learned in Egypt) and ground it to fine powder. He strewed the dust in the waters of the brook which descended from the mount and made Israel drink the bitter water of their sin. Then the old man toiled broken-hearted up the mountain for the sixth time, deeply conscious now of the cause of the divine anger, and the great pleader made his impassioned plea for forgiveness, offering himself in atonement if that were the only way. He was willing to be blotted out of the book of God for Israel's sake, a foreshadowing of the pleading of the nation's other kinsman in Romans 9:3.

Pleaders with God! Abraham interceding for the righteous in Sodom (Gen. 18); Moses for Israel and his own brother in particular (Deut. 9.19,20); Samuel for lamenting Israel (1 Sam. 7); Amos in the face of devouring locusts and fire (Amos 7.1-6).

The memory of the power these men had with God remained in the divine mind, so that centuries later the Lord said to Jeremiah, "Though Moses and Samuel stood before Me, yet My mind could not be toward this people: cast them out of My sight" (Jer.15:1).

Again the centuries passed and a lonely Man cried out in the sorrows of the Tree, "Father, forgive them; for they know not what they do". Then the darkness came down and the Pleader went into abandonment from God for the sin of the world, faintly prefigured in the desolate, sin-bearing scapegoat left alone to die in the wilderness. Then the resurrection morning saw Him ascend where He was before, and the Mediator from Calvary became the Advocate in heaven for all God's children, the High Priest for all His people, in a ministry of intercession which prevails against the charges of the accuser of the brethren. And so we sing:

Before the throne of God above

I have a strong, a perfect plea

A great High Priest, whose name is Love

Who ever lives and pleads for me.

God still searches among His people for pleaders, and the ministry of intercession; for brethren and sisters who, publicly and privately, will still fill "the golden bowls full of incense". He said to Israel, "I have set watchmen upon thy walls, O Jerusalem; they shall never hold their peace day nor night: ye that are the LORD's remembrancers, take ye no rest, and give Him no rest (Is. 62.6,7). Maybe someone reading this will say, from the heart fervently, "Lord, make me a watchman upon Thy walls, a pleader who will stand in the breach".

CHAPTER TEN:
OVERWHELMED

———

M any a dear saint of God has been overwhelmed. It is a very human experience, which knows no confines of time or space. At one time or another, in the lives of most, and even the most devoted, the heart is overwhelmed. It may be the reader is at the present moment.

The word "overwhelmed" occurs only eight times in our English Bible and each instance is in the Book of Psalms. Somehow this is not surprising, for to which other book does the heart so naturally turn in trouble? Luther called it "A Bible in miniature". Many of these precious psalms were written in days of affliction, to be read, century after century, by others experiencing similar difficulties. Similar, though probably quite different. It was often the persecution of enemies which overwhelmed the psalmists and that is sadly shared by many of our brethren in the world today. But for most of us it is the affliction of our circumstances.

Three different Hebrew words are translated "overwhelmed" in the eight occurrences:

KACAH, meaning to fill up or to cover. It occurs in Ps. 55.5 and Ps. 78.53.

SHATAPH, meaning to gush or to inundate. It occurs in Ps. 124.4.

ATAPH, meaning to shroud, as in darkness. It occurs in Ps. 61.2; 77.3; 102 (title); Ps. 142.3; 143.4.

(All meanings from Dr. Strong.)

These Hebrew words are translated into other English words elsewhere in Scripture, but for the moment we are only thinking of "overwhelmed", and in particular of ATAPH only - shrouded as in darkness. This is so real a description of the overwhelmed heart. The word occurs in five psalms, as noted above.

David wrote three of these psalms, 61, 142 and 143, the second being written "in the cave". Asaph wrote one of them, 77. But an unknown writer gave us 102. And in that anonymity many a dear Christian has seen himself or herself. It is "A prayer of the afflicted", in the darkness of his circumstances, the pouring out of his complaint before the God in whom he trusted.

Maybe the word "complaint" here gives a slightly wrong impression. The Hebrew equivalent is also translated "meditation". It comes from a root meaning to ponder, and by implication to utter one's thoughts aloud.

All unknown to others, many of God's children are, at this present time, calling on the Lord out of an overwhelmed heart; not necessarily complaining in their affliction, but simply in their deep inward musings calling out, "Why?" And no one understands better than the Lord Jesus. For He Himself called one day out of the darkness which enshrouded Him, "Why ...?" So He understands.

Maybe some overwhelmed heart, reading these lines, would like to take time to go through the five psalms referred to, that is 61, 77, 102, 142 and 143. If you do, the Holy Spirit will give you His own ministry from them, peculiarly and directly from Him to you in your own circumstances.

It may be in Psalm 61 the thought of the great Rock (v.2), the refuge, the strong tower (v.3), the covert of His wings (v.4) will bring comfort.

It may be in Psalm 77 a consideration of earlier experiences (v.6), a remembrance of help in past days (v.11), a meditation on His works, a musing on His doings (v.12) will bring cheer.

It may be in Psalm 142 the fact that God knows your path (v.3), that He is your refuge and portion (v.5) will bring strength.

It may be in Psalm 143 as you remember, meditate and muse (v.5), your overwhelmed spirit will so respond, as David's did, that you will say aloud to the Lord,

Cause me to hear Thy loving kindness (v.8),

Cause me to know the way (v.8),

Deliver me, O LORD (v.9),

Teach me (v.10),

Quicken me (v.11).

Take courage, overwhelmed heart. Fay Inchtawn put it choicely, doubtless having Genesis 45:27 in mind: "for o'er your bare, brown, hopeless hill, the wagons may be coming, nearer still."

They used to say, in the days of the shadows, "Thou hast beset me behind (the past) and before (the future), and laid Thine hand upon me (the present)" (Ps. 139:5). So all was well, and in those long past days overwhelmed hearts trusted Him. They came through fire and water is the strength of such promises as Isaiah 43:1,2: "But now thus saith the LORD that created thee ... formed thee ... redeemed thee ... called thee by thy name, thou art Mine. When thou passest through the waters, I will be with thee; and through the rivers, they shall not overflow thee: when thou walkest through the fire, thou shalt not be burned; neither shall the flame kindle upon thee".

But now the true light is shining, whereby we can say with even greater confidence, "And we know that to them that love God all things work together for good, even to them that are... foreordained ... called ... justified ... glorified" (Rom. 8.28-30). No wonder Frances Havergal, musing in life's latest hours on Jude verse 1, commented, "Called ... beloved... kept ... well I'll just go Home on that".

"Before us is a future all unknown,

A path untrod.

Behind us is a Friend, well loved,

That Friend is God."

CHAPTER ELEVEN: THE VOTE AND THE WHITE STONE

———

The Greek word 'psephos' is found only twice in the New Testament. It is translated "vote" in Acts 26:10 and "white stone" in Revelation 2.17. According to Dr Strong the word means basically "a pebble (as worn smooth by handling)". These pebbles were used for voting purposes. They were also used in the courts, "a white stone indicated acquittal, a black stone condemnation. A host's appreciation of a special guest was indicated by a white stone with the name or a message written on it" (Vine). There is thus an application of the word to a vote (as a citizen would record after a consideration of all the attributes or qualifications of a particular person) or to a verdict (as a jury would bring in after an assessment of all the facts).

Many a vote was cast against the early Christians. Fanatical Saul of Tarsus provided many cases for the biased adjudication of Israel's spiritual leaders. He went on his persecuting way, rooting them out of city after city, striving madly to make them blaspheme so that there might be a cast iron case against them of "death to the heretics". Yet, in the spirit of their Master, they did not resist him.

Paul says that in the court of the Sanhedrin, "I gave my vote against them" (Acts 26.10). That was his verdict based on the assessment of each case. In the case of Stephen, "Saul was consenting unto his death".

So the white stone was thrown in as vote and verdict against those faithful unto death Christians and from the court of human assessment they went by way of death to the court of heaven's assessment. "He that hath an ear, let him hear what the Spirit saith to the churches. To him that overcometh, to him will I give ... a white stone, and upon the stone a new name written, which no one knoweth but he that receiveth it" (Rev. 2.17).

These are the words of the Assessor of service on heaven's judgement seat. They refer to His verdict after considering all the facts, His vote after considering all the qualifications. And as those early Christians will hear on that Day the verdict and look on that lovely white stone with its new and secret appraisal-name, maybe they will remember another day when they were voted out of this world's society and relegated to the ranks and the pains of those worthy only to die. And they will rejoice for ever and ever.

The world still assesses the Christian and votes against him. Black stones are still being cast in. In some lands at the present time certain of our brothers and sisters in Christ are paying the supreme penalty of the unjust adverse verdict. God will judge their persecutors. In other lands the Christian is still being voted out from works and office circles and made to feel keenly the offence of the Cross. And in most cases they are doing it cheerfully, willingly, eagerly and sincerely.

What does it matter if we are voted out here so long as we are voted in there? How could the human verdict ever compare with heaven's white stone? What is the chaff to the wheat, the temporal to the eternal? Yes, it still stands written, "He that hath an ear, let him hear what the Spirit saith to the churches."

CHAPTER TWELVE: THE LESSONS OF KADESH-BARNEA

———

What is the lesson for the children of God today from the melancholy story of Kadesh-Barnea? (Num. 13,14). The hosts of Israel came out from Egypt, redeemed by the blood of the Passover lamb. It was a night of glorious deliverance, long to be remembered by the nation. The annual feast of the Passover was to ensure that it would never be forgotten. The waters of the Red Sea opened up in triumph before them, and they "were all baptized unto Moses in the cloud and in the sea" (1 Cor. 10.2).

In passing, it may be well to point out that we must not read into an Old Testament experience such as this any teaching for our own day which is contrary to New Testament revelation. For example, some have taught that since the children went through the Red Sea with their parents, so baptism today should not be withheld from the babes of believers. This amounts to reading into the type what is in fact contrary to the teaching of the antitype. In the New Testament, babes are not baptized by immersion, nor, of course, sprinkled by aspersion. New Testament teaching has in view the baptism by total immersion of disciples, believers who wish to "go on to know the Lord", in accordance with the great Matthew 28 commission. The word of all-authority is not to be diluted by human sentimentality.

Israel sang as they came from the waters of the Red Sea. It is the first recorded song of Scripture. There had been no song in Egypt. Now they sang the song of Moses. It was the song of a prophet who saw deep into the counsel of God. The nation was rejoicing in His works, but the leader was glorifying His ways. To him, the people had been redeemed with a view to being led and guided to the sanctuary of God (Ex. 15.13). So he bade them sing: "till the people pass over which Thou hast purchased. Thou shalt bring them in, and plant them in the mountain of Thine inheritance, the place, O LORD, which Thou hast made for Thee to dwell in, the sanctuary, O LORD, which Thy hands have established. The LORD shall reign for ever and ever" (vv.16,17,18). The people, the mountain, the place (Hebrew, a fixed appointed place), the sanctuary, the kingdom. It was an early vision of a grouping of Old Testament truths which would one day find a glorious counterpart in the spiritual truths of the New Testament.

From the Red Sea they journeyed by way of Mount Horeb. Moses kept a precise log of the entire journey from Egypt to Canaan, recorded in detail in Numbers 33. Forty-two times they journeyed and pitched.

It is impossible to trace most of the place names on a map for in all probability names were assigned to halting places which had some immediate significance (see e.g. Num. 11.34), but no permanent settlement was made. After some two years of journeying under the guidance of God, they came to Kadesh-Barnea. (The student will consider whether this was the thirty-second halting place of Numbers 33.) There, or thereabouts, the nation waited throughout the thirty-eight long, weary years of Deut.

2.14 - waited in unbelief - waited till a whole generation lay buried in the wilderness of wandering.

They had left Egypt in high spirits. If "the mountains skipped like rams, the little hills like young sheep" (Ps. 114.4), so did the people. The good tidings of Canaan, brought by Moses from the burning bush, were ringing in their ears. Now, at last, they were off to a good land and a large one, unto a land flowing with milk and honey. But the arch-enemy of all divine testimony was already hard at work, and he quickly destroyed the early vision of faith. As a consequence the nation plunged deep into unbelief.

When they reached Kadesh-Barnea they asked for spies to be sent to inspect and report. The Lord accepted their proposal. Twelve men set out and, of these, ten miserable sinners came back with an evil report which was in immediate correspondence with the doubting hearts of the tribes, and again they murmured. This was now the tenth time they had tempted God by their unbelief. This time He moved in swift judgement, swearing by the oath, "as I live", recorded here for the first time in Scripture. The ten spies would die; except for Joshua and Caleb the numbered of the nation from twenty years old and upward would perish in the wilderness and never see the good land; for forty years the people would wander, conscious of the alienation of God (see Numbers 14).

They were tragic years in Kadesh-Barnea; years of no consequence to God. The details of their happenings are passed over in the record of Moses. The despisers of the pleasant land were left to wander in their unbelief. Only Joshua and Caleb carried the inheritance in their hearts, waiting the day when they would enter into God's rest. The pathos of all this, the heartbreak to God, the warning to His children, runs through the Scriptures. David's graphic reference to it in Psalm 95 is taken up by the writer to the Hebrews and the teaching of Hebrews 3 and 4 calls for the serious study of God's children today. What then was the lesson of dark Kadesh-Barnea?

Scripture makes it clear that in Canaan was the place of God's rest. There He would indicate a specific place among the tribes where He would put His Name. It would be His habitation. To that place the people would come with their offerings. There they would do "all that I command you", a word twice repeated (Deut. 12.11,14). So the Lord planned to rest in the midst of an obedient people, and to make His house the place of His rest. But the whole adult generation that came out of Egypt failed to enter into this rest of God. They knew of it; heard of it in the word of good tidings; but failed to enter into it because of their unbelief. Redeemed? Yes. Baptized? Yes. But they never became associated with the place of God's rest.

One very obvious lesson for God's children today stands out from dark Kadesh-Barnea. According to 1 Corinthians 10 the story of Israel's journey from Egypt to Canaan is one great parable for us and the happenings in the way were typical experiences from which we should learn important lessons. Thus many of the redeemed of the Lord today go forward into baptism; having become "united with Him by the likeness of His death", so they are "also by the likeness of His resurrection". That is excellent for it is in accordance with the Master's word

(Matt. 28.19), apostolic practice (Acts 2.41), disciples' experience (Acts 18.8) and doctrinal significance (Rom. 6.4).

But this step is only a first step. In Israel's case (and it happened to them as an example to us, as witness 1 Cor. 10.6) the redeemed (Ex. 12) and baptized (Ex. 14) were to be guided onward to God's holy habitation (Ex. 15.13), to be planted in the mountain of divine inheritance, the place where He dwelt, the sanctuary He had established (v.17). They were to "enter into My rest" (Ps. 95.11). Where God ruled, they were to live as a subject people.

And so it was in New Testament times. The redeemed and baptized presented themselves for reception into one of the churches of God (see e.g. Acts 9.26). Together, these churches were in the one Fellowship of His Son, Jesus Christ our Lord (1 Cor. 1.9). The individual church was "a habitation of God in the Spirit" (Eph. 2.22). The fellowship of churches ("each several building, fitly framed together" RV; "all the building" KJV) and was a "holy temple in the Lord" (Eph. 2.21). This was the place of God's rest. To those gathered disciples He committed the Faith, which embodied the teaching of the "all things" of Matthew 28.20. It was delivered to the saints, not for criticism, consideration or compromise, but for obedience. As a consequence God found rest in His house. He ruled in His kingdom.

And so it is today. The call comes to the sinner in the gospel. In his response he will find redemption. But it is a continuous call. The faithful preacher will tell him of baptism. If he responds he will rise to walk in newness of life with his new Leader. Teachers faithful to the Word should then show him the seven steps of Acts 2.41,42. God is still calling. If he responds he will take his place in a church of God and thus find himself in the spiritual house of God. He has reached it in the pursuit of the response of faith to revealed truth (some alas, may never have it revealed to them, never see it). There he is taught to "lay aside every weight, and the sin which doth so easily beset us" and to "run with patience the race that is set before us" (Heb. 12.1). The spirit of obedience to God's Word, which brought him to the place of God's rest in His house, is required of him during the years of his association with it.

May the Lord enable readers to reach the present-day counterpart of Canaan, indicated above, and not to experience the lost years of Kadesh-Barnea. And may He fill us all with such complete confidence in the Word of His grace that we shall not only reach the present-day experience of the rest of God in His house but in it experience also the power of Christ resting on us.

CHAPTER THIRTEEN: THE GUEST CHAMBER

The Shunammite was "a great woman". A holy man of God was passing by continually and she saw the need to show him hospitality. She suggested to her husband that they make "a little chamber in the wall". He agreed, and that little chamber with its bed, table, stool and candlestick became the resting place of Elisha, the man who "poured water on the hands of Elijah". A guest-chamber for one of the weary of God's people; and a choice setting for Peter's gem in 1 Peter 4.9, "Using hospitality one to another without murmuring". What a delightful work of age-long pleasure to the Lord, dating it may be from even earlier times than Genesis 18 when even angels were entertained unawares! May the mounting "cares of the world" be prevented from choking this gracious exercise among us today.

There was a guest-chamber in the upper flat of a Jerusalem home (Luke 22.7-13). In its New Testament setting the Greek word 'katafumo' signifies (a) an inn, lodging place, Luke 2.7; (b) a guest-room, Mark 14.14; Luke 22.11. The word literally signifies a loosening down ('kata': down, 'luo': to loose), used of the place where travellers and their beasts untied their packages, girdles and sandals (W.E. Vine). As an inn the word is used exclusively in association with Immanuel's resting place on the night of His coming into the world. As a "guestroom" it is used exclusively of His resting place on the last night of His pilgrimage here.

The Jerusalem guest-chamber was in a very real sense that night the place of unloosening. Peter and John had followed the instructions regarding the man bearing a pitcher of water. "Go ... meet ... follow". His menial action was indicative also of the grace of the other Man they followed. And during supper the Lord Jesus rose, laid aside His garments, girded Himself with the towel, then washed the disciples' feet. We are thankful for Peter's protest for it brought from the Lord the delightful teaching of the two kinds of spiritual washing. But beyond all, we are deeply grateful for the Master's example in the sphere of gentle lowliness. "I Am" was still in the midst of His people. but here "as One that serveth". So He unloosed His garments, served, and then took His garments again in a love which loved to the uttermost.

But in addition, the Jerusalem guest-chamber was the scene that night of an unloosening in a spiritual sense. It was the unloosening of the dispensations. For the last time the Lord kept the Passover, nor do we read of His disciples ever keeping it again. It had been the great yearly act of remembrance in the era of the first Covenant; but that Covenant was now growing old and would shortly vanish away. And during the Passover supper the Lord instituted the Breaking of the Bread. That was to continue as the great weekly act of remembrance in the era of the New Covenant until His return. So after sunset, in the early hours of the day He died; it was as though the Lord, the Framer of the ages, unloosed the old dispensation and brought in the new. Honoured guest-chamber indeed, and honoured "good man of the house"!

CHAPTER FOURTEEN: THE GLORY OF THE LORD

"And the Word became flesh, and dwelt among us (and we beheld His glory, glory as of the only begotten from the Father), full of grace and truth" (John 1.14).

It was the day of all days when the Word, the eternal, became flesh. This mystery of godliness is very great. The heathen monarch spoke of "the gods, whose dwelling is not with flesh" (Dan. 2.11). But this was our God manifest in flesh. This was the coming of the Only Begotten from the Father; as from alongside Him. When Israel called amid the troubles of Egypt, the LORD answered them "in the secret place of thunder" (Ps. 81.7); so the thunders of God shook Egypt. But when the whole creation groaned and travailed in pain together, the response was heard "in the bosom of the Father"; so from the Father, in supreme gentleness, the eternal Son came down to sojourn among us for our help and salvation.

"The heavens declare the glory of God" (Ps. 19.1). The LORD shone forth from Mount Paran and "His glory filled the tabernacle" (Ex. 40.34). In the temple of Solomon, "everything saith, Glory" (Ps. 29.9). But there was a manifestation of the divine glory which was both unique and complete, when the Son came down. John, who saw it, put it so simply and reverently, it was the glory of the only begotten from the Father.

Not, of course, that the disciples saw the glories which radiated from Him in the excellency of the Father's presence. These He had laid aside in the self-emptying of Philippians 2.7. But there were other glories of deity seen by them. They are said to have witnessed the first manifestation of His glory at Cana, when the "simple wedding guest" did to water what only almighty God could do. Six other similar manifestations deeply impressed John and he dealt with each in his Gospel. To him they were signs of the glory of God as seen in the beloved Son, glories peculiar to deity.

Yet there were other glories in the Lord's person seen by His marvelling disciples; great moral excellencies. Writing years later, John tells of the earliest and perhaps deepest impression which his Master made on him, "that God is light" (1 John 1.5). The sinless purity of the Lord profoundly affected both him and his fellow disciples, Simon Peter expressing it this way, "Depart from me; for I am a sinful man, O Lord" (Luke 5.8). They had seen in Him the glory of sinlessness. They watched His sympathetic handling of the multitudes and saw the glory of compassion. They marvelled at His gentle dealings with those who were slow to learn and saw the glory of patience. They saw the affection which He poured out on His tormentors and saw the glory of love. The reader may well take a little time and ponder many more glories besides. This was "the glory of God in the face of Jesus Christ" (2 Cor. 4.6).

Seven times Moses, the servant of the Lord, went up Sinai to speak with God. On his final descent "Moses wist not that the skin of his face shone by reason of His speaking with him" (Ex. 34.29). For forty days he had been listening to the voice of his

God. Now he was reflecting as a mirror, consequently yet all unconsciously, the glory of the Lord. With his great spiritual perception, Paul through the Spirit takes up the point and develops it in a very choice way in the setting of the New Testament era. He spells out the contrast between the two eras, yet points to the same basic principle applicable to both.

Tables of stone - now tables that are hearts of flesh.

The Old Covenant of the letter - now the New Covenant of the Spirit.

The ministration of death and condemnation - now the ministration of the Spirit and righteousness.

The glory which was passing away - now the glory that surpasses and remains.

The veiled face of Moses - now we all have unveiled faces.

Surely we live in a glorious day! And as we make our spiritual ascents to the holy mount; as, like Elijah or Gabriel, we stand in the presence of God; and as, like Moses, we hear His voice coming live to us today from the living oracles of Scripture, we too may begin to reflect the glory of the Lord (2 Cor. 3.18). We ponder the story of that winsome Man and consider the excellence of His moral glories. He said, "Blessed are the poor in spirit". He was poor in spirit. Again He said, "Blessed are the meek". He was meek. "Blessed are the merciful". He was merciful. "Blessed are the pure in heart". He was pure in heart. "Blessed are the peacemakers". He was a peacemaker.

And as we meditate on one such individual glory of the Lord's character, we may proceed to assimilate it and then reflect it in our own lives, consequently but maybe quite unconsciously. Then by the Lord's help we may proceed in our study to another aspect of excellence in the Lord's most glorious life, until that too is in measure assimilated and reflected in our life. Thus we may enjoy the experience described by Paul in the words, "But we all, with unveiled face reflecting as a mirror the glory of the Lord, are transformed into the same image from glory to glory, even as from the Lord the Spirit". And from our hearts which were once darkness, light shall stream out; reflected light; beaming out "the glory of God in the face of Jesus Christ".

Thus, one choice aspect of the glory of God which was seen in the character excellencies of the person of Jesus Christ in the days of His earthly walk, will be lived out again and seen in the person of His followers today. To Him be all the praise and glory.

Then one day we shall go to see His glory, in its every delectable aspect. It was to this the Lord referred in His prayer. It was a dark night with, humanly speaking, no visible glory. The nation had repudiated Him and on the following afternoon would give expression to this with venom and scorn. Many of His followers had found His teaching too deep and demanding and had turned back to walk no more with Him. Yet there were hearts that loved Him. Maybe they started off by thinking He was on His way to an earthly throne and glory, and they with Him. But gradually they had begun, perhaps with tear-stained eyes, to see things differently. They were trying hard to understand the Cross, and trust Him for everything. That night there seemed no glory, as men count glory - just a borrowed room, and a penniless Leader whose sole possession appeared to be a garment without seam. But they saw in Him the glory of God and were content. How He loved them for their simple faith. He could well picture what it was impossible for them to envisage, the glory He had left, the added glory in and to which He would within a few days return.

He prayed, "Father, that which Thou hast given Me, I will that, where I am, they also may 'be with Me; that they may behold My glory, which Thou hast given Me: for Thou lovedst Me before the foundation of the world" (John 17.24). Little wonder we sing sometimes:

Comfort of all my earthly way,

Jesus, I'll meet Thee some sweet day;

Centre of glory Thee I'll see,

Wonderful Man of Calvary!

It may be a very little while till we all go Home to see the beloved King in His beauty, in the far-stretching Land which once He left for our sake. In that day we shall be "conformed to the image of His Son" (Rom. 8.29). Today is our opportunity so to yield ourselves to Him that, here and now, we shall be "transformed into the same image from glory to glory, even as from the Lord the Spirit" (2 Cor. 3.18). Challenging contemplation.

CHAPTER FIFTEEN: AS HIS CUSTOM WAS

It was the habit of life of the carpenter's Son to enter the synagogue at Nazareth every Sabbath day and hear the Scriptures read and expounded. Luke says, "as His custom was" (Luke 4.16). It was not that He might Himself expound. When at length He entered on His public ministry the people of Nazareth marvelled. The Carpenter they knew had never ministered as now He did. But though He had never ministered, He had never missed. "Wist ye not that I must ..." was His attitude at the age of twelve. It was the habit of His life to attend.

The silent years passed and He went forth to do the Father's will. The multitudes came together to Him "and, as He was wont, He taught them" (Mark 10.1). It was now the habit of His life to teach. Again we read, "And He came out, and went, as His custom was, unto the mount of Olives ... and prayed" (Luke 22.39-41). It was the habit of His life also to pray.

Is then a disciple above his Master or a servant above his Lord? Is it not still enough for the disciple to be as his Master and the servant as his Lord? Does not the principle of the upper room still hold good, "If I then, the Lord and the Master, have ... ye also ought"?

Paul evidently thought so. When Luke describes his coming to the synagogue at Thessalonica he says that Paul "as his custom was, went in unto them". He had been commissioned to take the gospel to the Jew first, so in every city he sought them out. It was the habit of his life.

As we write, and read, many of us will recall the habit of life of those who in our formative years and since, perhaps unconsciously, helped to mould our lives in this connection. It was their custom never to miss the gathering of God's people, whether it were Lord's day meetings, weeknight meetings, special meetings or conferences. They were not simply motivated by the desire to inspire others. They loved these gatherings, and besides were they not following a Master whose custom was never to miss?

The local assembly may not be large or particularly gifted, but we remember that the young Carpenter must have sat year after year patiently listening to inadequate exposition. So we must accept the Master's example and renew our zeal. "Not forsaking the assembling of ourselves together, as the custom of some is" (Hebrews 10.25) is one of the age-long principles of the Faith. Even in those early days it had evidently become the lamentable habit of life of some to absent themselves without cause from assembly gatherings. "Let us therefore draw near", whether it is the hour of worship or prayer (Hebrews 10.22, 4.16). Let the people of God in the house of God make it evident that in their several priorities the gatherings of the saints have an unchallenged place. Naturally it is not always possible for all to be at all the assembly gatherings. But what is the overall habit of our lives? In retrospect, will it be said of us, "As his custom was"?

CHAPTER SIXTEEN: THE MYRHH

———

The shepherds brought the Babe no gift. But the wise man from the east brought Him gifts, for was not God's name great among the Gentiles? So falling down and worshipping the young Child, they opened their treasures and offered their gifts. There was gold, and frankincense and myrrh.

There was gold for the King-child; thus wherewithal to carry the holy family on the long journey to Egypt and sustain them there. There was frankincense, carrying fragrance for One who would become the praying Man who would make intercession for the transgressors. But there was myrrh for the Man of sorrows. The late Mr McGaw would, on occasion, amend the carol, and say,

My myrrh I bring with its bitter perfume,

Tells of a life of gathering gloom;

Sorrowing, sighing, bleeding, dying,

Laid in a stone-cold tomb.

Yes, all His garments smelt of myrrh, as He took our infirmities and carried our diseases. And when He came at last to Calvary, it was to Him like the mountain of myrrh of which Solomon had written. And there "they offered Him wine, mingled with myrrh". The lonely Sin-bearer was tasting death, in all its bitterness, for every man; making Himself of no reputation. Well did the poet sing,

Who shall fathom that descending,

From the rainbow-circled throne,

Down to earth's most base profaning,

Dying desolate alone?

"And they made His grave with the wicked, and with the rich in His death". In the Hebrew text "the rich" is singular. So in precise fulfilment of the sure word of prophecy "there came a rich man from Arimathea, named Joseph"; and with him Nicodemus "bringing a mixture of myrrh and aloes, about a hundred pound weight". So the Babe to whom the myrrh was brought from afar, who grew up in its daily fragrance, was finally wrapped in myrrh in His manhood - the Man of sorrows laid in a tomb.

But the sufferings of Christ must be followed by His glories. How beautifully Isaiah depicts the coming day of Messiah's manifestation, when Gentiles will come again to His light and their kings to the brightness of His rising. In that day in Israel's land "the multitude of camels shall cover thee, the dromedaries of Midian and Ephah; they all shall come from Sheba: they shall bring gold and frankincense (Isaiah 60.6). Yes, gold and frankincense but no myrrh in that day. The sufferings are all past. The days of Israel's mourning shall be ended (v. 20) - and His too.

Myrrh - suffering - threaded through all our lives. But no sorrow in the land we are going to. Little wonder the apostle reckoned, "that the sufferings of this present time are not worthy to be compared with the glory which shall be revealed to usward". It may be, as we write, you are experiencing sorrow of varying hue, suffering of varying degree, dark clouds hanging low. But it will all pass, enriching us on its way. Then sooner perhaps than we realize, He that cometh shall come, and in our case also the days of our mourning shall be ended.

From vintages of sorrow are deepest joys distilled,

And the cup outstretched for healing is oft at Marah filled.

God leads to joy, through weeping; to quietness, through strife;

Through yielding, unto conquest; through death, to endless life.

CHAPTER SEVENTEEN:
TITHING AND GIVING

Old Testament tithing

The origin of the tithe is lost in antiquity. We can say with assurance however that the giving of the tenth to God is an ancient procedure. Abraham observed it in the rather special circumstances of Genesis 14.20 and Jacob promised it to God in the first vow in Scripture, that is Genesis 28.22. In both cases it was "a tenth of all".

Some centuries later God recognized the nation of Israel as His people, and gave them His comprehensive law. In this, for a particular purpose, He specified His minimum requirements from the substance of His people. To this they might add any amount of freewill offerings. The basic minimum was the tithe, the tenth part of the individual's annual business increase. This increase related to the seed, the fruit, the herd and the flock, as in Leviticus 27.30-32.

This tithe, or its monetary equivalent as in v.31, had to be handed over at the house of God in the Place of the Name (Deut. 12.5,6) with joy and feasting. It was the Lord's portion, holy unto Him, and God was robbed if it was not presented (Mal. 3.8).

The reason for the tithe was that the Levites had no inheritance in Israel's land and God's provision for their substance was:

(i) In the case of the priestly family, their portion was "all the heave offerings of the holy things which the children of Israel offer unto the LORD" (Num. 18.19).

(ii) In the case of the Levites, their portion was "all the tithe in Israel for an inheritance in return for their service which they serve (Num. 18.21). From this tithe the Levites had to offer the tenth part to the Lord as a heave offering (vv.25,26).

The tithe of all the increase of every third year was required by the law to be handled in a different way. Instead of taking it to the house of God, the Israelite had to lay it up at home, to be distributed to the Levites, the stranger, the fatherless and the widows who lived nearby, after which he would go to the Place of the Name and there record his gratitude (Deut. 14.28, 29; 26.12-15).

One further point may be selected as relevant to tithing generally. Only the tenth part of the best was worthy of God. For example, Abraham (Heb. 7.4) gave a tenth from "the chief spoils" ("primarily the top of a heap" - Vine). In Israel's case the tithe was "of all the best thereof' (Num. 18.29).

So far we have considered what was mandatory in Israel. The tithe took care of the needs of the Levites, the priests and the needy among the people. That was all. Israel had no expenditure on outreach to the other nations. They were a people who in that sense, "dwelt alone".

New Testament giving

Here the picture changes. The mandatory element of the law disappears. Grace now reigns in giving as in all else. Yet the old principle remains - only the best is worthy of God. We lay out now some of the scriptures in which the Holy Spirit has given certain principles backed up by actual experiences as general guidance for disciples in the churches of God:

Romans 12.8 – "he that giveth, let him do it with liberality."

1 Corinthians 16:2 – "let each one of you lay by him in store, as he may prosper."

2 Corinthians 8:3 – "Beyond their power, they gave of their own accord."

2 Corinthians 8:12 – "if the readiness is there, it is acceptable according as a man hath, not according as he hath not."

2 Corinthians 9:6 – "he that soweth bountifully shall reap also bountifully."

2 Corinthians 9:7 – "let each man do according as he hath purposed in his heart; not grudgingly, or of necessity: for God loveth a cheerful giver."

Philippians 4:18 – "I am filled, having received the things that came from you, an odour of a sweet smell, a sacrifice acceptable, well-pleasing to God."

The givings referred to here were in general collections taken in the churches on the first day of the week. They were in response to the needs of brethren engaged wholly in the extension of the Lord's work such as Paul and Barnabas, and to the needs also of fellow-saints in the churches who were in financial distress, such as occurred in the churches of Judea. There was a very close parallel between the needs met by Old Testament tithing and New Testament giving.

But the New Testament giving was not tithe-bound. It was rather, as the above verses indicate, according as the saints prospered and purposed; given ungrudgingly, spontaneously, cheerfully and liberally, even to the point of additional hurt to some already in poverty. It was all as "unto the Lord" in appreciation of the "unspeakable Gift" of God which had so enriched them.

Such then briefly was the spirit of giving under grace. The question of tithing did not arise. Love in reciprocity simply met the need, whatever the cost. And as it was then so will it be by the urge of the Spirit today. The people of God are not tithed. They are not restricted in their giving in response to need and to the ongoing demands of the Lord's work. Yet some readers might be stirred in their response were they to compare what they give financially to the Lord with what amounts to one tenth of their income. It is all a matter of personal exercise in the Lord's presence, but pressing nevertheless.

CHAPTER EIGHTEEN: THE REPAIRER OF THE BREACH

The "ifs" and the "thens" of Isaiah 58 make most instructive reading and the description of restored Israel as "the repairer of the breach" is altogether choice. It contemplates a regenerated people, delighting at last in the Lord and choosing gladly the things that please Him, spreading her benign influence over the nations in that coming day of Messiah's glory.

But it had not always been so with Israel. Throughout her national history there had been many and sore breaches in the hedge around her vineyard, all of them brought about by the wayward pursuits of the people. They forsook the God of their fathers; made light of the covenant of their ancestors; loved the ways of the nations. The people themselves were the first cause of the breach.

But in addition there was no corrective, remedial ministry from the main stream of the teachers to whom the people were prepared to listen. Israel had two kinds of teachers; those who spoke to them from the heart of God and those who spoke to them "out of their own heart". As time went on the latter increased and had the ear of most in the nation. According to Ezekiel 13.4,5 these teachers failed in two particular ways. In the first place they did not go up "into the gaps" (or breaches, RV margin). In the second place they failed to make up "the fence for the house of Israel, to stand in the battle in the day of the LORD". So they neither stood in the breached fences nor did they repair them. Thus Israel was left increasingly open to enemy attack with, as a consequence, no "strength to them that turn back the battle at the gate" (Is. 28.6).

Finally the crisis came in the eleventh year of Judah's last king, Zedekiah, when the enemy came from Babylon and "a breach was made in the city" (2 Kings 25.4). The divine record is full of pathos. "And I sought for a man among them, that should make up the fence, and stand in the gap before Me for the land, that I should not destroy it; but I found none" (Ezek. 22.30). Marvellous forbearance; a God still willing to be entreated by a pleader, if only one could be found; remembering another day, and a better one for Israel, when "Moses His chosen stood before Him in the breach, to turn away His wrath, lest He should destroy them" (Ps. 106.23).

Breaches can still be made by the Lord's people today; some which affect the fellowship of the disciples between themselves; others which affect the strength of the house of God in its testimony to the world. It is so easy to make them; not so easy to repair them. A hasty word, a thoughtless act, and an offence is given which breaches fellowship between disciples and may take years to heal. Even spiritual death may ensue; or a separation dropped, an association formed, and the testimony of the people of God is weakened.

Therefore God still looks for breach repairers. He will find them today just where He missed them in Israel. He will find them among those who minister in His house the living oracles of God; men who in their teaching instruct the Lord's people faithfully as to all holy living and godliness; with an ongoing, upbuilding, knitting together, envigorating, enriching ministry. And by means of it breaches are healed here and prevented there.

He will find breach repairers also among the people. These are the disciples who, sinned against by another, go faithfully to the offender with the authority of Matthew 18.15 and in the spirit of meekness "shew him his fault between thee and him alone: if he hear thee, thou hast gained thy brother". Or again, there are those who themselves first made the breach with another disciple; and conscious of it go on the instruction of Matthew 5.23 and seek reconciliation with the one they may have deeply hurt. Or again, there are those who see fellow disciples err concerning some aspect of the truth. In the gentleness of Christ they approach them for their help, till they walk again the separated path with the Lord's people in harmony with His will.

Yes, it is easy to breach; to hurt, offend, give the enemy a victory. Not always so easy to repair; to heal, restore, win over, pull back from the edge. But it is very well pleasing to the Lord; and in the remedial effort yet another name goes down on the divine record, as it is written "And thou shalt be called, the repairer of the breach" (Is. 58.12); maybe also one day to be "graven on the white stone in Immanuel's land".

CHAPTER NINETEEN: THE IMPLICATION OF "THE DECREES"

We refer to Acts 16.4. The implication of the decrees was that no church of God is wholly autonomous, that is, self-governing; and that what affects one church may affect all others. The Greek word used for decree is 'dogma'. "It primarily denoted an opinion or judgement ... hence an opinion expressed with authority, a doctrine, ordinance, decree" (Vine).

The decrees in Acts 16.4 arose out of the circumcision problem affecting the Gentile disciples in Antioch. Certain brothers came down from the Church of God in Jerusalem, and contrary to the mind of the apostles and elders there, taught in the Church of God in Antioch, "Except ye be circumcised after the custom of Moses, ye cannot be saved" (Acts 15.1).

Now there were spiritually-minded leaders in the church in Antioch, as evidenced in Acts 13.1, men perfectly capable of handling the problem within their own assembly. They could have argued, as is done by so many beloved brothers today, that they were responsible for the conduct of the affairs of their own assembly, and no other assembly had the right to intrude. But none knew better than these leaders, and the assembly itself, that they did not stand alone in testimony. In Acts 14.27 Paul and Barnabas had already told them of the new assemblies which had been planted by them during their missionary journey, and of the extension in this way of the fellowship of churches into Gentile territory, of the growth of the kingdom of God, of the holy nation.

They rightly concluded that the teaching brought by these brothers from Jerusalem was rank heresy. But they foresaw that were they to judge the false teachers and prohibit their teaching in the church, the men were perfectly capable of creeping in privily elsewhere and other churches with whom they were in fellowship would be exposed to the same evil. They thought "imperially". They considered what steps should be taken to ensure that all the churches would be authoritatively advised how to deal uniformly with this problem.

So they decided to send to Jerusalem certain men, including Paul and Barnabas, to confer with the apostles and elders in the church there. It is suggested that first there was a private discussion between the brothers from Antioch and the leaders who were of repute in Jerusalem, as shown in Galatians 2:2, but we do not pursue here the significance of this action. Then they were received of "the church and the apostles and the elders" (Acts 15.4).

This was the Church of God in Jerusalem. It had grown to be a vast congregation, as the early chapters of Acts show (Acts 2:41;4:4,32;5:14;6:1,7). Few, if any, would contend that all this multitude of disciples could gather for assembly services in the one place. They must of necessity have met in many companies (for example, see Acts 4:23; 12:17). Yet it remained one church, referred to e.g. in Acts 5.11 as "the whole church", and had one group of elders as we have noted in Acts 15.4.

We find it hard to understand in this connection why so many believers who are loosely associated with other similarly minded believers in other companies in the same town, regard each company as self-governing under the guidance of its own elders, and ignore the obvious scriptural requirement that all the companies should form one church in the city, under one united elderhood. What has happened to the New Testament pattern?

After the welcome meeting by the church in Jerusalem, the apostles and elders gathered together to consider the principles involved in the Antioch problem and what the counsel of the Holy Spirit would be in the matter. In due course they came to one mind and agreed on a certain course of action which should be followed in the ever growing number of Gentile churches. The details of this course of action were "the decrees". And when Paul and Barnabas, accompanied by two of the chief men among the brethren in Jerusalem, brought the letter to the church in Antioch, the disciples there "rejoiced for the consolation".

And now we come to the point which concerns us, that is, the implications of these decrees. After a brief spell, Paul and Silas set out on a tour of the Gentile churches, passing through Syria and Cilicia, then on into lower Galatia. "And as they went on their way through the cities, they delivered them the decrees for to keep, which had been ordained of the apostles and elders that were at Jerusalem. So the churches were strengthened in the faith and increased in number daily" (Acts 16.4,5).

All this is detailed by orderly Luke as a true record of divinely authorized procedure in the early churches and his record has been preserved by God for all time and, in particular, for ours. Not only did all the companies of disciples who were obedient to the Faith in a city form one church of God there; but that one church was also under one united elderhood; moreover that one church was non-autonomous; and we see also that as the Faith of our Lord Jesus Christ was being increasingly revealed, it was held in common sacred trust by all the churches of God for they were in one Fellowship, one Community.

Today the Faith has been once for all delivered to the saints; delivered for safe custody; and for contention if necessary where its principles are being eroded. And we believe that one of these erosions has been the lack of perception of what was involved in "the implications of the decrees". This is a matter which calls for serious reflection by many beloved fellow believers today.

CHAPTER TWENTY:
WATCHMEN ON THE WALLS

———

Watchman is an Old Testament word. The New Testament spiritual equivalent, overseer, may be detected in Isaiah 56.9,10.

It seems there were always watchmen on the walls of ancient cities. There are two most dramatic references to these in Isaiah 21. The first was Isaiah's prophetic vision of the night of Belshazzar's feast, so tersely summarized in verse 5. By the word of the Lord a watchman was set on Babylon's wall, instructed to declare what he saw. Day after day he watched from his tower till at last he saw the advance of troops of Median horsemen. He cried out: "Babylon is fallen", and "in that night Belshazzar the Chaldean king was slain. And Darius the Mede received the kingdom" (Daniel 5.30,31). He received it from the hand of the Lord.

Again, in verses 11,12, in the burden of Dumah (probably Idumea) one called to the watchman on sentry duty on the wall of Seir (probably Edom), "Watchman, what of the night? Watchman, what of the night?" What time is it, or, what is left of the night? But the watchman's response was enigmatic, then silence, in keeping with the meaning of Dumah, silence. "The morning cometh, and also the night: if ye will inquire, inquire ye: turn ye, come". Edom's future was dark with the judgements of God (Ezekiel 35) and the watchman on the wall saw only gloom ahead for an unrepentant people.

There are three Hebrew words translated watchman. One of these means to peer into the distance; the other two mean to protect or guard. So the function of the watchman was to look intently outward and ahead with a view to protecting and guarding the people within the city. There were always watchmen on Zion's walls, as evidenced, for example in 2 Samuel 18.24-26, Isaiah 52.8 etc. Not only so, but God set watchmen within the city among His people as, for example, in Jeremiah 6.17. These watchmen were described by Isaiah as God's shepherds keeping watch among His flock (Isaiah 56.10,11).

But in Isaiah's day the watchmen-shepherds were "blind, they are all without knowledge; they are all dumb dogs, they cannot bark; dreaming, lying down, loving to slumber ... these are shepherds that cannot understand: they have all turned to their own way, each one to his gain, from every quarter". Little wonder the nation was so completely immersed in sin, so totally away in heart from the Lord. The watchmen-shepherds had no understanding of their responsibilities. They only thought of themselves and not of the well-being of the flock. They could not "bark" and thus warn, for they dozed away in their sloth while moral and spiritual declension swept through the nation and carried it to the point of "no remedy". Yet in it all, the people had to bear the punishment of their own sin.

But even in the land of their captivity the divine principle still held good, for God appointed Ezekiel as His watchman there (Ezekiel 3.17). His terms of reference were clear. It was his responsibility to warn the chastened nation on the appearance of any departure from the Lord or His Word. If he saw the danger and remained silent he would be held responsible by the Lord. If he did warn and no one heeded he was exonerated and the people held responsible. "Thou hast delivered thy soul". The whole principle of the responsibility of the watchman was elaborated later in most solemn detail in Ezekiel 33.1-9.

Watchmen on Zion's walls - with what sense of expectancy we cast our minds forward to the fulfilment of Isaiah 62.6-9 and consider the watchmen on Zion's walls in preparation for the day of Messiah's glorious reign. "... they shall never hold their peace day nor night: ye that are the LORD's remembrancers, take ye no rest, and give Him no rest, till He establish, and till He make Jerusalem a praise in the earth". Pattern watchmen indeed!

We now consider briefly how this relates to our day. The watchmen in the New Testament churches were clearly the overseers, the Greek word being 'episkopos', from 'epi', over, and 'skopeo', to look or watch. They were the watchmen on the walls, whose responsibility was to guard the spiritual well-being of the people of God in their churches. The word to the disciples in Hebrews 13.17 was, "Obey them that have the rule over you, and submit to them: for they watch in behalf of your souls, as they that shall give account; that they may do this with joy, and not with grief: for this were unprofitable for you".

The word translated watch in this verse means literally 'to be sleepless (from 'agreuo', to chase, and 'hupnos', sleep)" and "is used metaphorically, to be watchful" (Vine). Contemplated here were the New Testament watchmen overseers who indeed "took no rest"; men who "had a knowledge of the times" and were carefully observant of the tactics of the adversary outside, and of any signs of departure from the word of the Lord among the people inside; men who looked also to the future and detected in the shape of things to come what might adversely affect the holy nation under their care. Here were men who would avoid the sin of Israel's watchmen-shepherds, who for their own selfish ends loved to lie down drowsily dreaming, men who failed to "bark" in the face of impending danger, who failed to warn because their dulled minds had become insensible to evil.

It is all a powerful reminder for both the watchmen-overseers and the people of God watched over today. The Holy Spirit uses the illustration of watchmen who are watchful to the point of sleeplessness in their anxiety for those under their care. He envisages overseers who are able to discern the adverse impact on the saints of the devices of the evil one, as he walks round the churches seeking where he may intrude and devour. The tactics vary from saint to saint. The spectrum of temptation is broad and menacing. But watchful overseers are responsible to warn and not to remain silent.

Or it may be that within the church the watchmen overseers can see worldliness creeping into the lives of individual saints; or a failing interest producing apathy; or a faith which is faltering under temptation; or some practices being proposed which would mar the unity of the holy nation. Whatever form it takes it is a menacing danger from outside or inside the walls and again the watchmen elders must speak out, privately in some cases, publicly in others, and warn the people of God.

Or again, the future may hold dangers which are evident to observant watchmen. The increasing all-round collapse of moral standards is insidious to even the best conditioned disciple; nor have the saints an immunity against the deeply heretical statements made by certain national church leaders. Further, the spirit abroad today of reaction against the established principles of law and government can subconsciously affect the mind of a disciple who would normally recognize rule in God's house. Whatever it is, when the watchmen on the walls foresee danger for the spiritual lives of the separated people of God, they must speak out in plain words of clear scriptural guidance. If not, they will be held accountable by the Chief Shepherd at His coming.

But with the saints themselves lies a deep responsibility to respond to the counsel, the warnings of their watchmen elders, for their spiritual safety. It is on their behalf that the elders watch and speak. The day of accountability by these elders to the Chief Shepherd is fast approaching. It will be the time of His Judgement Seat. And if they give verbal account with grief (and this assumes their own faithfulness in having given warning) then it will be unprofitable for the saints involved. Truly it will be well for the elders and those under their care if the relationship between Paul and the Thessalonians will be true of them in that Day: "For what is our hope, or joy, or crown of glorying? Are not even ye, before our Lord Jesus at His coming? For ye are our glory and joy" (1 Thess. 2.19,20).

CHAPTER TWENTY-ONE: THE STAR

I t was a star which, at the first, shone over Bethlehem, for it was there the Babe was born. Was He not Messiah the Prince of whom Daniel and the prophets had written? Was He not Emmanuel come to earth to be of the house and family of David, the one-time King of Israel? So the shining star brought the Magi from the East, seeking. And the prophetic word of Micah the Morashtite was fulfilled through the counsels of the world ruler, Caesar Augustus, to bring Joseph and Mary to Bethlehem, waiting (Micah 5.2).

It was a long road from Nazareth to Bethlehem; but the Bethlehem road was rich in memories of other days, some sad, some joyful. It had been a pathetic road for Rachel, a bitter road for Naomi, but a thrilling one for David's intrepid men as they made for the well. They came from different directions; all had different experiences. And there, at Bethlehem, "Mary brought forth her firstborn son."

Why was there no room in the inn? Why should Emmanuel be laid in a cattle manger? We wonder. Maybe just the census throngs. But there comes to mind, with deep significance, what John saw in Patmos as the great drama of the conflict of the ages was unfolded to him, involving Satan in his unremitting, but utterly unavailing, efforts to destroy the purposes of the Lord God the Omnipotent. "And the dragon stood before the woman which was about to be delivered, that when, she was delivered, he might devour her child. And she was delivered of a son, a man child, who is to rule all the nations with a rod of iron: and her child was caught up unto God, and unto His throne" (Rev. 12.4,5).

So Mary's Babe was safely delivered, and to the woman Israel a Child was born that day, a Son was given. Thirty days later the happy parents took the Babe to the Temple in Jerusalem. It was a lovely scene - Mary, so poor that for her ritual cleansing she could only offer "a pair of turtle doves or two young pigeons." A lamb was beyond her means; yet, as has been pointed out, she carried the little Lamb of God in her arms. And she had in her hand the five shekels (Num. 18.16), with which to redeem her little One, yet He was Himself the world Redeemer. What a presentation to the Lord!

Then back to the little temporary home in Bethlehem. Unknowingly, the Magi followed them, the star which they had seen in the East going with them. Then it stopped, stood over the house where the young Child was, and they entered with their gifts. The shepherds had brought no gifts to the Babe. Israel was to reject Him. But the Magi brought gifts, for the Gentiles would one day welcome Him. So, opening their treasurers, they offered Him gold for a King, frankincense for a Man of prayer, myrrh for a Man of sorrows.

But the gold was God's provision against the next tactical move of His adversary. The enraged Herod, frustrated by the departure of the Magi "another way," set himself to ensure the death of "the young Child." But all unknown to him, he was simply paving the way for the family move to Egypt, so that Hosea's prophecy would in due course be fulfilled, "I ... called My son out of Egypt" (Hosea 11.1). And they left behind them "Rachel weeping for her children," just as Jeremiah had foreseen (Jeremiah 31.15). So the gold would suffice for the visit to Egypt.

Then came the recall and the long journey back to Galilee. The prophets had written that the young Child should be called a Nazarene, and one by one the long succession of divine predictions were reaching fulfilment. So He came back to Galilee; back to the Galilee He was going to love and live in during His brief stay in Manhood; back to the Galilee where mountain and lake were to draw Him again in resurrection days.

CHAPTER TWENTY-TWO:
THE LAMP

———

The lamp began to burn in Israel. It was a burning and a shining light. It appeared for a little time then burned itself out. The lamp was John. the uniquely given son of Zacharias and Elizabeth. That little family, with their related family in Nazareth, together with Simeon and Anna, formed the new nucleus of eight souls, part of the small godly remnant of Israel with which the New Testament opens. They have been likened to the eight basic notes of music, the great octave, from which the whole melody of Christian testimony has been developed.

Normally John would have become a Temple priest, following his father in the circuit of sanctuary service, after the order of Abijah, that being also the eighth to come forth by lot in 1 Chronicles 24.10. But the great prophecies of God overruled all normal circumstances. What a moment it must have been in the silence of the Holy Place in the Temple of God, Zacharias probably alone before the altar of incense, when the heavenly visitor suddenly stood at his side, saying, "I am Gabriel, that stand in the presence of God; and I was sent to speak unto thee!" Tremendous moment in human history. The forerunner of Emmanuel was about to be born. Messiah the Prince would shortly be on His way.

Thus there came to Israel a man sent from God. All that we know of his early years is that he was with God "in the deserts till the day of his showing to Israel." While Messiah the Prince was in preparation in a carpenter's home and shop in Nazareth, His forerunner was also in preparation, but he was seemingly alone with his God in the wilderness of Judea. Then the great day came when God showed him to Israel; and a lamp began to burn on the banks of the Jordan. It was a hot, burning lamp, yet clear-shining. Hot, burning, for he was the fearless voice to Israel of the last and greatest of all her prophets. denouncing sin and calling the nation to repentance. Clear-shining, for he left no one in doubt as he gave his personal testimony to the fact that the Son of God was now in their midst, as the gentle Lamb of God walking in and out among them.

There must have been a marvellous bond of affection and mutual understanding between the forerunner and Messiah the Prince. For a period John alone baptized and multitudes flocked to him. The nation for a season rejoiced in his light. He laid no claim to being the prophet of whom Moses had spoken, nor the Messiah of whom the prophets had written. So the leaders left him alone. But Messiah the Prince, in the very nature of things had to appear, and the forerunner would require to give place. His disciples sensed the effect of this and sadly, yet understandably, drew his attention to the transition in the hearts of the people. John's reply was characteristically large-hearted in its loyalty. "I am not the Christ, but ... I am sent before Him. He that hath the bride is the bridegroom: but the friend of the bridegroom, which standeth and heareth Him, rejoiceth greatly because of the bridegroom's voice: this my joy therefore is fulfilled. He must increase, but I must decrease" (Jn. 3.28-30). Truly, noble words.

Then came the confrontation with Herod the tetrarch when the fearless Baptist denounced him for his moral transgression in the matter of his brother Philip's wife. So he bound in prison a man whose righteousness was as conspicuous as Herod's wickedness, and later beheaded him at the instigation of a wicked, unforgiving woman. "And his disciples came, and took up the corpse, and buried him; and they went and told Jesus" (Matt. 14.12) The voice by Jordan was silenced. The lamp had burned itself out in Judea.

CHAPTER TWENTY-THREE:
THE LIGHT

———

Not till the lamp went out by Jordan did the "great light" begin to shine in Galilee. Not till Jesus heard that John was delivered up did He begin "to teach and to say, Repent ye; for the kingdom of heaven is at hand." The whole setting is choicely laid out in Matthew 4:12-17.

First, He left Nazareth in the heart of Galilee's south country, and made for the sea. There were fishermen there, and from them He would call, discipline, train a few. And Isaiah's vision would begin to find fulfilment, "My disciples ... Behold, I and the children whom the LORD hath given Me are for signs and wonders in Israel from the LORD of hosts, which dwelleth in mount Zion" (Is. 8:16-18).

So He came and dwelt in Capernaum, in the borders of Zebulun (Hebrew: 'zabal', he dwelt) and Naphtali (Hebrew: 'niphtal', he wrestled). The words in brackets are in the RV margin of Genesis 30.8,20. Messiah the Prince was among His people, dwelling, preaching, healing. He was also among His people, wrestling, day after day striving against sin, not His own. But He was striving against Satan His adversary, whose works He had come to destroy. Whittier has well described what may have been the feelings of the people in those fragrant days:

The healing of his seamless dress

Is by our beds of pain;

We touch Him in life's throng and press,

And we are whole again.

While we for our part may enjoy another verse from the same poem,

But warm, sweet, tender, even yet

A present help is He;

And faith has still its Olivet,

And love its Galilee.

There, in Galilee of the nations, the Galilee despised by Jerusalem, "the people which sat in darkness saw a great light, and to them which sat in the region and shadow of death, to them did light spring up." The true Light was now shining in the darkness of Israel. Nor could that darkness, nor all the power of its prince, overcome or extinguish it. Even in the darkness of Calvary the true Light put off from Himself the attacking principalities and powers of the rulers of the entire world's darkness. And that "great light" from Galilee, now the Light of the world, has shone ever since from the firmament of grace, and will continue to shine, more and more, till the "perfect day."

And He is still looking for lamps, burning and shining lamps, lamps which are prepared either to burn on and out for Him, or go on shining till He returns. "Seeing it is God that said,

Light shall shine out of darkness, who shined in our hearts, to give the light of the knowledge of the glory of God in the face of Jesus Christ" (2 Cor. 4.6). He has shone in, to give light. Not to us, but to others. He has shone in our hearts so that light may now stream out from whence there was once darkness only - torches in broken pitchers (Judg. 7.20), if you like; or light reflectors as in the church in Philippi (Phil. 2.15): lamps, burning with a strong warmth of affection to those who sit in darkness; shining with a clear illumination of the great truths for which we stand in the defence of the whole counsel of God. Again, another poet put it searchingly:

His lamps are we

To shine where He shall say;

And lamps are not for sunny rooms

Nor for the light of day

But for dark places of the earth

Where shame and wrong and crime have birth;

Or for the murky twilight grey

Where wandering sheep have gone astray;

Or where the lamp of faith burns dim

And souls are groping after Him.

CHAPTER TWENTY-FOUR: BATTLING DISCOURAGEMENT

———

This, of course, was no foe to faith's princely Leader, the Lord Jesus, of whom it was written, "He shall not fail nor be discouraged" (Is. 42.4). What a choice contemplation never failing, never discouraged! It was not as though the tide failed to flow swiftly against Him. He had enemies, defecting followers and unfaithful disciples. He was misunderstood and misrepresented. He was finally repudiated and rejected. Yet at no point was He discouraged - remarkable thought! Inwrought into this was the fact that at no time was there any personal failure. His life was cast in the mould of His Father's will, and He unerringly completed, day by day, the work which had been given Him to do. So His serene mind was unaffected by daily adversities and in this joy His great strength lay.

But with us the position is quite different. We are so slow to take on the character of our Leader. Unlike Him, we fail, and because of this we become discouraged. Indeed this may well rank among the chief reasons why the hands of many of God's children hang down or their feet turn out of the way. Sheer discouragement - and then they give up the struggle. We take comfort that some of the great men and women of faith of all ages have battled their way against this same adversity. Discouragement is an intensely human failing, and profoundly weakening. In this, the mighty Elijah, who towers among the pinnacles of faith, showed himself a man of like passions with us. He stood habitually in the divine presence, controlled the rain at his word, condemned the sin of the house of Ahab, challenged and slew the prophets of Baal then dejected and discouraged fled to the wilderness and "requested for himself that he might die". He felt he was the last of the line. "I, even I only, am left". He was discouraged by a sense of loneliness.

This can be most weakening. It may affect us from several causes. The assembly may be small and the hard core smaller still. There may be few at the prayer meeting, some too busy with trivial things. Or again, loved ones may have gone, one by one, from the home and there are vacant chairs. Maybe few call to pass an hour of friendship. From whatever cause, we are cast down, oppressed by a sense of loneliness. And then we remember that lovely, lonely Man of Galilee, who, now on God's throne, understands completely, for He passed this way. We think also of how we have innumerable fellow-members of the Body who are everywhere experiencing a like lot; of how also we have been called into the Fellowship of His Son, Jesus Christ our Lord, so that there is an even closer "fellowship with hearts to keep and cultivate". And we thank God, and take courage.

Then there may be a sense of personal unfulfilment. The last words of Cecil Rhodes were reputedly, "So little done, so much to do". And we think of the years passing over us with so little apparently to show for our personal witness. We just have to face this and not run from it. "I have found no works of thine fulfilled before my God" was the warning to Sardis. So we sense failure and grow discouraged. Better far to have a frank examination of our manner of life and seek by the Lord's help to rid ourselves of anything which may be impeding the flow of the Spirit through us to others. Then gather encouragement from Isaiah's call, "Strengthen ye the weak hands, and confirm the feeble knees, say to them that are of a fearful heart, Be strong, fear not" (Is. 35.3-4); glorious words, picked up and pointedly applied by the writer to the Hebrews (Heb. 12.12-13).

So let us do what we can with a will, after the manner of our Leader, of whom it is written, "The zeal of Thine house hath eaten Me up". Mr J. C. Radcliffe used to quote to our delight in younger days, "Do what you can, being what you are; you can be a glow-worm if you can't be a star". And, says Jeremiah, "Refrain thy voice from weeping, and thine eyes from tears: for thy work shall be rewarded, saith the LORD" (Jeremiah 31.16). Well did the Holy Spirit say for our encouragement, "Your labour is not vain in the Lord".

This leads to another source of discouragement; in this case it may also be collective in its impact - a sense of lack of blessing in the assembly. This can be spiritually devastating to those who appreciate their high collective calling, appointed to "go and bear fruit, and that your fruit should abide" (Jn. 15.16). The spiritual impact of the assembly in the vicinity of the meeting room may be visibly reducing. Useful personal contacts with those outside may be thinning out. Numbers in the children's and youth work may be at a low ebb. The open-air witness seems ineffective and little if any response detected from the quantities of literature given out. Generally there are few being saved and fewer still discipled. Fruitful soil indeed for a thriving weed of discouragement.

Nor is there any modern short-cut by means of which we may weed it out. The assembly must go to the Lord about the matter, strong in their understanding as to what is required of us in the moral and spiritual sphere if prayer is to be effective. Not only so, but avenues of assembly outreach must be explored afresh. Overseers and deacons must carry a basic responsibility for this, but the saints generally are involved.

Indeed from the exercised younger people may come suggestions as to openings for the Word which are well worth exploring. These all require study in the fear of the Lord as to their suitability in relation to God's house. A fresh appraisal of how best the assembly may take on the character of casting down strongholds is called for. Some fresh, approved feature may help considerably the gospel service; a new approach to various age groups in children's and youth work; openings for contact with the lonely, the aged, the sick; meetings in houses where the doors of friends or neighbours are opened. Whatever we do, let us not give up by reason of discouragement, nor, on the other hand, fall into the trap of substituting entertainment for evangelisation.

Then again we may be cast down from a sense of the Lord's chastening hand. As He loves, so He chastens, and always for our good. Sometimes it is irksome; always, to the exercised, profitable. It may be we are not yet wholly committed, and He touches us in some way so that on self-examination a more dedicated person may emerge. Or we may be in danger of overmuch self-esteem and again He touches us so that a better sense of proportion will develop. Whatever it is, from a position of seeming strength we go into temporary weakness, so that in the purpose of the Lord we may rise to greater and purer spiritual power. And it is when we are thus weak that the danger of discouragement is present.

Paul was conscious of it. By reason of the greatness of the revelation granted to him, there was also given him a thorn in the flesh, a messenger of Satan to buffet him, lest he be exalted overmuch. He might have felt discouraged, dejected. Actually it was only to be one of his many weaknesses, injuries, necessities, persecutions, distresses for Christ's sake. But Paul went to God about the matter. From Him he learned the secret. There was no need to be weak, no need to be discouraged, for through these very experiences the power of Christ could rest upon him. There he said, "when I am weak, then am I strong".

Time would fail to consider in detail another matter which affects so many of us, that is a sense of general despondency. Sometimes disciples in whom we had placed our hopes turn back and walk no more with us. And we have recourse for comfort to the Lord's own long look at His retreating followers in John 6.66, or to Paul's steadfast spirit at Miletus despite the wolf-cries in his ears, as described in Acts 20.29.

Or it may be God-fearing parents silently mourn over children who have, at least for the present, broken the family togetherness in spiritual things. And the weary hearts grope through tears for the promise of Jeremiah 31.16. Or it may be the frequent mocking of those who cast doubts into even the strongest minds as to the need for separation in its many aspects if the whole counsel of God is to be given effect to. And our hearts yearn for an unquenchable faith which will bear us along in the path of the revealed will of God, until, without major regrets, we shall one day, please God, look back and say, "I have fought ... finished ... kept".

And so Bunyan wrote, "Now they went on; and when they were come to By-Path Meadow, to the stile over which Christian went with his fellow Hopeful, when they were taken by Giant Despair, and put into Doubting Castle, they sat down, and consulted what was best to be done; to wit, now they were so strong, and had got such a man as Mr Great-Heart for their conductor, whether they had not best to make an attempt on the Giant, demolish his castle, and if there were any pilgrims in it, to set them at liberty, before they went any further. So one said one thing, and another said the contrary. One questioned if it were lawful to go on unconsecrated ground; another said they might, provided their end was good. But Mr Great-Heart said, 'Though that assertion offered last cannot be universally true, yet I have a commandment to resist sin, to overcome evil, to 'fight the good fight of the faith'; and, I pray, with whom should I fight this good fight if not with Giant Despair? I will therefore attempt the taking away of his life, and the demolishing of Doubting Castle.'

"Then they fell to demolishing Doubting Castle, and that you know might with ease be done, since Giant Despair was dead. They were seven days in destroying of that; and in it, of pilgrims, they found one Mr Despondency, almost starved to death, and one Much-Afraid his daughter; these two they saved alive. But it would have made you wonder to have seen the dead bodies that lay here and there in the castle yard, and how full of dead men's bones the dungeon was."

Finally, and for our help - the sons of Korah sang, "Why are thou cast down, O my soul? and why art thou disquieted within me? Hope thou in God: for I shall yet praise Him, who is the health of my countenance and my God" (Ps. 42.11). David, in a day of profound distress, when lesser mortals would have been discouraged to the point of giving all up, "encouraged himself in the LORD his God" (1 Sam. 30.6 KJV).

Fay Inchfawn, a poetess of recent years, when she thought about these things was directed to Genesis 45.27, and comforted the fainthearted with the words, "For o'er your bare, brown, hopeless hill, the waggons may be coming, nearer still." Yes, we may not have long now to hold on in the face of discouragement, unconquering it may be, but, by God's grace, unconquered. And there comes vividly to mind brother Alan Toms telling an audience of Indian Christians of a missionary who was returning home on furlough. It had been a long, tough assignment. The ship was nearing the home port. There were many on board, pleasure bound, business bound, and many more to welcome them on arrival. But there was nobody there to greet the toiler from the field. He too might have been discouraged, till he heard an inward Voice say, "Son, you're not home yet".

Soon shall the cup of glory

Wash down earth's bitterest woes;

Soon shall the desert brier

Break into Eden's rose;

The curse shall change to blessing,

The name on earth that's banned

Be graven on the white stone

In Immanuel's land.

Did you love *Wisdom from a Watchman*? Then you should read *The Power of Prayer* by Guy Jarvie!

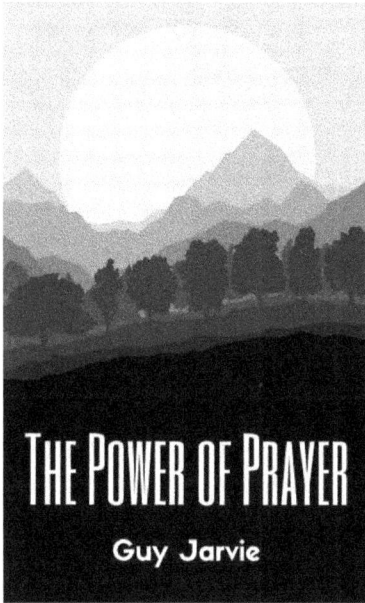

Guy Jarvie was a missionary who spent much of his time in Myanmar (Burma) and countless hours in the practice of prayer. This book comprises his writings on the subject which occupied so much of his life.

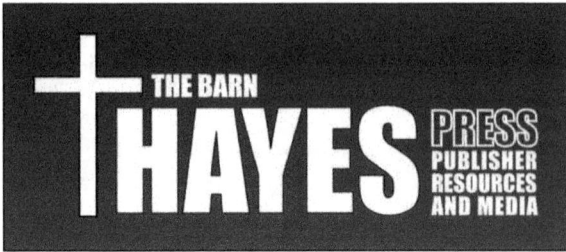

About the Publisher

Hayes Press (www.hayespress.org) is a registered charity in the United Kingdom, whose primary mission is to disseminate the Word of God, mainly through literature. It is one of the largest distributors of gospel tracts and leaflets in the United Kingdom, with over 100 titles and hundreds of thousands despatched annually. In addition to paperbacks and eBooks, Hayes Press also publishes Plus Eagles Wings, a fun and educational Bible magazine for children, and Golden Bells, a popular daily Bible reading calendar in wall or desk formats. Also available are over 100 Bibles in many different versions, shapes and sizes, Bible text posters and much more!